A ROMANY ON THE TRAIL

A ROMANY ON THE TRAIL

G. BRAMWELL EVENS

WITH ILLUSTRATIONS BY G. K. EVENS

ISIS
LARGE PRINT
Oxford

First published in Great Britain 1934
by
The Epworth Press

Published in Large Print 2005 by ISIS Publishing Ltd,
7 Centremead, Osney Mead, Oxford OX2 0ES
by arrangement with
Mrs Romany Watt

British Library Cataloguing in Publication Data
Evens, George Bramwell, 1884–1943
  A Romany on the trail. – Large print ed.
  (Isis reminiscence series)
  1. Natural history – Great Britain
  2. Country life – Great Britain
  3. Large type books
  I. Title
  508.4'1

ISBN 0–7531–9314–0 (hb)
ISBN 0–7531–9315–9 (pb)

Printed and bound in Great Britain by
T. J. International Ltd., Padstow, Cornwall

A ROMANY ON THE TRAIL,

in which Raq and I re-introduce you to

JOHN FELL	*Gamekeeper*
JERRY	*Poacher*
ALAN AND JOE	*Farmers*
NED	*Village Postman*
JOHN RUBB	*Angler*
SALLY STORDY	*Cottager*

CONTENTS

CHAPTER
ONE

The Care of Young Birds

Passing by a cottage I heard Jerry's well-known voice. Walking round to the back Raq (my spaniel) and I found the old poacher and Davie Hope, one of the village boys, looking at what appeared to be a rabbit-hutch.

"Davie 'ere 'as got an increase in t' family," said Jerry smiling.

"Four on 'em," added Davie proudly.

Looking into the hutch, I saw four young guinea-pigs, mottled in black, brown, and white, their little noses twitching with curiosity as they examined the wonderful world into which they had come.

"Last neet," Davie went on, "the big 'uns were a'reet, an' this mornin' I come doon and 'eard squeakin', and found 'em wi' four little 'uns runnin' aboot."

"And what did ye expect to find them doin'?" asked Jerry.

"I thowt they'd be lyin' in a nest, same as young rabbits. I never thowt they'd be as wick as yon so soon after they were 'atched oot."

"Well," said Jerry, with a smile, "be careful 'ow ye 'andle 'em, Davie. Ye've only to pick 'em up once by their tails fer their eyes to drop oot, and then all t' king's 'osses and all t' king's men won't put 'em back agin. So be careful now."

Davie grinned broadly, and yet I could see affection for the old poacher lying behind it. "I reckon it ud tak' better eyes nor I've got to find any tails," he said.

When we got away on the road together, I said to Jerry, "I must own I was a bit surprised to see those young guinea-pigs running about and feeding, and only born

an hour or two. If you had asked me I should have said that they were born in a nest, and stayed there for a week or so."

"Speakin' in a gin'ral way, animals which is born blind and 'elpless allus 'as a nest protected-like, somewhere oot o' sight, up a hole in a 'edge-bank, or under the roots of a tree. Young rabbits is born blind an' naked, so is young voles an' otters — so ye find t' mother rabbit scoopin' oot a 'ole under t' field, an' th' otter finds a place under t' river bank where no eyes can see 'em. But them as is born in the oppen —"

"Like young hares," I interrupted.

"Aye," echoed Jerry, "young 'ares 'as to be ready for takkin' care o' theirsels pretty quick, and so they're born more forward-like. Hi! Raq, come 'ere with yer."

2

I heard the thudding of hoofs in the field we were passing, and looking over the hedge saw Raq near a mare and a young foal. It was clear that the mare did not like the presence of the dog, and had put herself between him and her foal.

"It's a lanky young beggar," I said as Raq obediently returned when I whistled.

Jerry nodded. "An' when yon youngster were foaled its legs would be almost as long as its mother's, the reason bein' that 'osses is grazers, and when they've shortened one patch o' grass, they allus 'as to move on to find more food. I'm talkin' of when they was in their wild state, o' course. T' foals 'ad to move on wi' 'em, so Nature gives 'em long legs to start wi' so as they can keep up wi' their parents. Most animals as feeds on grass brings long-legged little 'uns into t' world."

"I'd never thought of that. Cows and deer, of course."

One field of hay we came to was only partially cut. The rain had evidently interfered with the mowing, and there was left quite a large patch of grass still standing in the middle of the field. From it there came the curious grating voice of the corn-crake. "Crake, crake" — "crake, crake." So Jerry and I crouched down in the hope of seeing it.

"When voices was given oot I reckon yon bird got a job line," said Jerry with a grin. "There were two on 'em one year just behind me cottage winder, and some nights they fair drove me crazy wi' their clock-windin' voices. 'Ave ye ever seen one?"

I nodded. "But I've never really had a proper view of one."

"Well, 'ere's yer chance. Put Raq through yon standin' grass, and one on us 'll stand on either side. T' chance is that she'll mak' fer yon 'edge; so leave 'er that way to get oot."

So we took up our positions, and the dog was soon ranging about in the standing grass. Once I thought I saw the shape of a small brown head peering above the stems, but it was only for the fraction of a second. A moment later it rushed up on the wing, and, as Jerry had surmised, was soon lost from sight in the hedge.

"She flies like a water-hen does, with her legs dangling. I almost thought she'd fall, she was so poor a flier, wasn't she?"

"Aye, ye'd think she were a bit of a mug at it, but yon bird actually crosses t' Atlantic when autumn time comes roond, an' she dodged you reet enough, old man," and Jerry patted Raq.

"Anyway, she doesn't waste much energy flying whilst she's in this country, Jerry. Have you ever found her nest?"

He nodded. "Aye, but not often, though I've never set mysel' seriously to look fer one. Them as I've seen I've gin'rally come across as I were ratchin' roond casual-like. They was i' patches o' rank grass and nettles, and sometimes in a field like this yin."

"And what happens to the nest if the hay harvest is an early one, and the bird has hatched out late?"

"Then she's got to tak' 'er chance o' the cutter makkin' mincemeat of 'er chicks. I've 'eerd it said as

4

'ow that is why t' corn-crake is gettin' rarer. In th' old days grass used to be cut by hand, and then she 'ad a chance o' leadin' away 'er chicks to safety afore the scythes could touch 'em, but not wi' t' mowin'-machine."

"I hope it isn't true that corn-crakes are dying out. They are not too common as it is. Are you sure of it, Jerry?"

"Let's 'ave a smoke an' give Raq a chance to see what 'e can find," was Jerry's answer. We found a resting-place at the foot of a mighty oak. "There's nowt I likes better 'n to 'ear t' rustle o' wind in a full-leaved tree."

"You haven't answered my question yet about the scarcity of the corn-crake," I reminded him after a bit.

"Well, it's not easy-like to find an answer that'll satisfy all roond. When ye've lived in t' country as long as I 'ave ye'll find that nearly all birds 'as their good seasons and bad 'uns. I recollect t' days when t' lanes were wick wi' goldfinches, an' other years ye couldn't find one. A few years sin' ye could walk all day in t' marshy fields and niver see a redshank. To-day ye can find  a dozen or two wi'in a mile or so. It's just like trade — it comes an' goes."

We sat in silence for a moment or two watching a flock of starlings.

"Tak' them starlings fer instance," went on Jerry. "Them's increasin' at a big rate. Ye can hardly find a hole in a barn or tree which 'asn't 'ad a nestful o' young uns. But their lean time'll come. Nature seems to let 'em go on prosperin' fer 'ears, and then she'll wipe 'em oot wi' some disease or other. Then another kind o' bird'll get its chance. Every dog 'as 'is day. So wi'in a few years, mebbe, t' corn-crakes 'll be flourishin' agin."

As Raq scrambled through the hedge there was an angry clamour at his intrusion. A moment later a young bird hopped out from the hedge and sat a few yards off, looking at us wonderingly, yet without fear.

"Young thrush," I said.

"Young blackie," Jerry corrected.

I looked again more carefully, and saw that Jerry was right.

"I ain't surprised ye said thrush," said Jerry; "it's oncommonly like one."

"The spots on its breast were so clearly marked, like a young thrush's. It was brown, not black," I said.

"Aye, but it just proves what I've telled ye afore. Thrushes and blackbirds come o' th' same stock. They're relations, so to speak. I'll show ye summat to mak' ye understand what I mean."

So we tramped along by the fields where the poppies glowed blood-red in the sun, and the yellowhammer chanted his one little phrase from the hedge. Once Raq put up a partridge family, but the little fellows were on the wing in time and could just manage to flutter away, a little unsteadily, it is true, into the next field.

"Let 'em enjoy their life. Their fun ends wi' th' guns i' September," was Jerry's comment.

We paused at last before a hawthorn hedge, and peering into a nest, Jerry said, "What is 't?"

"By the colour of the eggs I should say a thrush's, but by the nest lining of grass I should say a blackbird's. But the eggs are cold."

"Aye, she's deserted it fer some reason or other, but I saw 'er sittin', and I know it's a blackie's."

He pulled the old nest from the hedge and held it in his hands as he spoke.

"T' blackbird is t' same as thrush's, but she's improved it by linin' it wi' grass on top of the mud. Then she's improved 'er song — it's conversational-like, not scrappy like a thrush's. But they're relations reet enough, and so ye finds young blackies born brown, instead of black, and wi' marks o' the thrush on their breast still showin'. But ye niver saw a young thrush born black."

"No, that's true, Jerry. How curious."

"An' what's more, a blackie sings same as a thrush, but ye niver 'eard a thrush singin' them grand flute-like notes of a blackie, did ye?"

"So you really mean that the blackbird is an aristocratic relation of the thrush?"

"Aye, ye've only to notice the 'aughty way 'e cocks 'is tail up to see that."

CHAPTER
TWO

Night Fishing

"Half past nine at the shop." I knew well enough what this message from John Rubb meant.

Home I hurried to get my fishing-tackle ready, and by half past nine we were speeding out of the town, Raq in the back seat of the car, as usual.

We saw several anglers as we neared the river.

"That's Short, minnower," said John as we passed one man. There was a certain amount of scorn in the last phrase. To designate a man a "minnower" or "wormer" always provokes the scorn which a fly-fisherman has for one who uses as bait either minnows or worms.

I listened to John with much amusement and came to the conclusion that in the fishing world each man is known by the cast he uses. And speaking generally, he will only go fishing when the river is in the condition which suits his particular style — dirty water for "wormers" and water "clearing off" after a spate for "minnowers."

"Did you see yon feller looking over the bridge?" John asked as we climbed a hill. "That was Billy Clarkson." I knew him by repute to be one of the worst poachers in the district. He not only knew the position of every salmon lying in the river, but knew how to fettle up an old kelt, a spawned salmon, so that it looked almost like a salmon fresh run from the sea.

"When he gets a kelt with his gaff, how does he fettle it up, John?" I asked.

John chuckled. "Oh, they say he fetches a drop of blood from the slaughter-house and pumps it into the kelt somehow. Ye know when ye cut a salmon, if it's in good condition the blood ought to foller the knife. Then he gets a drop of ink and makes it a nice dark blue-green shade on the back — and there you are. Then he sells it to folks who like a bit o' good salmon at sixpence a pound."

"And if the 'river-watcher' finds him at his game, what then?"

"Of course he's been caught red-handed a few times, and been up before the magistrates, but it's in his blood. His father was a poacher before 'im, and I reckon his son knows every inch of the river, too. He's escaped from the river-watchers many a time by swimming right across the river."

We parked the car in its accustomed place, with the pine-trees for a roof, and having "tackled up," walked slowly towards the river with Raq at our heels. The sky was a deep indigo, though in the west a pale silvery light still lingered. From the middle of the fields, as we passed, the rabbits scuttled back to their burrows, their tales bobbing like tufts of white cotton. Over some of the meadows we heard the "Hoo, hoo, hoo," of the tawny owl — "the bogey-man of all wee beasties," as John called him.

As we neared the river, a bird with a very raucous voice scolded us for disturbing the sanctuary.

"That's a sedge-warbler," said John, "a bird that never sleeps. I pass those reeds all hours of the day and night, and allus find he's got something saucy to say. What is he like? Oh, a small brown bird, light brown underneath, and darker brown on top, with a line running from his bill to the back of 'is head. He's a born acrobat. He can climb on the reeds just like a tomtit hangin' on to branches. But he's a right uneasy bird. Tread quietly," he added, as we neared the bank. "It's the vibrations our feet make stampin' on the ground as warns the fish there's someone about."

"You don't think they can hear us talking, then?"

John shook his head. "Only things with ears is sensitive to sounds, an' a fish, if ye notice, hasn't any. It don't need to sing a love-song to its mate, or call out warnings as birds do. No, they can't hear us talk, but you've noticed the bone that runs from the gill to the tail? Well, that's their sensitive receiver — like one o' them instruments that records earthquake shocks."

"A seismometer," I suggested.

"Yes, that's the thing. Often when I've been lying quiet on a bank watching the fish in clear water I've noticed that they take no notice of a cow walking down to drink, but if they hear a human footfall they flash into their hidin' places quick."

"What fly shall I use to-night, John?" I asked, as we separated to fish adjacent pools.

10

"It doesn't really matter which particular one you use for night fishing, but I always like one with a bit o' silver on its body, so that it flashes a bit as it moves." Here John opened his fly-case and showed me his marvellous selection. "I prefer this ghostly one better than this one with bushy wings. Trout, I find, seem to like a frail, fluffy one better than a thick stodgy mouthful."

Here he paused and raised a warning finger. "Don't wade in the river more than you can help. All the big fish come into the shallows to feed at night. They daren't come there in the day-time. They choose a spot not in still water, but just where the main current tails off."

"Tight lines," he said, leaving me.

Raq sat on the bank hour after hour watching me fish. From time to time he would stamp with his forepaws on the bank — one way he has of reminding me that he is tired of waiting, but will tolerate it a little longer. Just when I was interested in some slight pull at the end of my line, a yelp and a squeal stabbed the

silence in a most unearthly way. I hurried out of the water to see what was the matter. I found that Raq had killed a large rat, and that blood was flowing freely from the tip of his nose. Putting my tackle down, I ferreted in

11

my pocket for iodine, the only thing I had with me. I wondered what had made him attack the rat, for as a rule he is not interested in such creatures. Probably it was passing, and he had put his nose down to investigate. He then received the surprise of his life — and so did the rat.

I sat for a few minutes on the bank to allow the water to settle again. All I could hear was the sound of John's cast whipping through the air. Once I heard the unmistakable flop of a hooked fish, as it made its first two or three rushes on feeling the hook.

"Want any help?" I called, picking up my landing-net.

"I think I can manage, thank you. I've got his measure all right," was the reply; "but he's makin' a game fight fer his life."

So I slid back as gently as possible into the water again. Except for the tinkle of the stream against my waders nothing could be heard, though once I thought I heard the churring note of the nightjar as she hawked for moths.

Then came that slow decisive downward pull at my line that I had been waiting for so long. I gave a slight flick of my wrist upwards, and the next moment, before I had time to call "Got him," a fine sea-trout leaped like a silver crescent right out of the water, and then went back with a fine splash.

"You're into a good 'un," called John. "Give him plenty of line. Lower the tip of yer rod if he jumps out again or he'll break yer tackle."

My reel was screaming out in unending fashion as the fish carried it out further into the river, so I put the gentlest of pressure on the line by letting it run between my thumb and forefinger.

"That'll make him stop and think." It did, for he turned and rushed towards me like lightning, and it was as much as I could do to reel in my slack line. But when at last I tightened it up again I was relieved to find that he was still on the other end of it. John came over to me, as it rushed up stream again, and peering into the dark waters, said, "Give him a bit of yer rod. If he has the strength of the stream and your own pressure on him he'll soon tire." And so he did. Soon the rushes grew feebler, and I felt I had the mastery.

As I pulled him gently towards where John stood waiting with the landing net, I noticed Raq rushing about excitedly on the bank. From long experience he knows what patience anglers need, and the signs of luck when they do come. The fish turned on his side. Putting the net underneath him, and taking great care not to touch my cast, John flopped the sea trout into the net.

"Three-and-a-half pounds, if it's an ounce," said he excitedly as we edged our way to the bank, "and you played it well." This last praise gave me as much pleasure as the catching of the fish, for John is an expert angler.

"Poor thing. I wish we could catch them without killing them, John," I said. "You know I always regret taking life."

"Now, don't go talkin' like that, or you'll be giving up fishin' as you have done shootin'. That sea-trout was takin' life when you caught him. He'd have swallowed any number of minnows, and they in their turn were on the look out for worms and flies, and so on."

As we sped homewards, John said, "I heard a yarn the other day to suit you."

"Go on," I said encouragingly.

"In a small village on the banks of a good fishing river, the parson and most of his congregation were all very keen anglers. One week evening during a service in the chapel the door opened and the newcomer whispered audibly to a man in the back pew, 'Salmon's up,' then out he went. A moment or two later the man in the back pew got up and went out. So the news went round, and one after another the congregation slunk out. This was really more than the parson could stand, so he said, 'Look here, friends, I'll pronounce the benediction, and then we can all start level.'"

CHAPTER
THREE

Hay Harvest

"It's a long time sin' I clapped eyes on ye," said Sally Stordy by way of greeting.

"You were out the last time I passed through the village," I said. "At least your door was closed. I suppose you were out doing somebody a good turn."

"And when would that be?" she asked.

"Last Friday week."

"Last Friday week," she murmured thoughtfully, "that was t' day afore oor old soo pigged. Aye, I was oot reet enough, I were up at Emma Braisby's, she's bin ailing a bit lately, so I thowt as I'd go and fettle up things fer 'er."

"So you've got a litter of young pigs, have you? How many are there?" I asked.

"Fourteen, an' all livin' an' well," she answered proudly. "Like to 'ave a look at 'em?"

We went out through the back kitchen, and made our way to the sty. I could hear the squeakings of the youngsters, and as we neared the sty the old sow showed that she recognized Sally's step by giving an expectant grunt.

I leaned over the gate and watched her preparing to lie down on her side.

"This isn't another Sarah Ann, is it?" I asked, remembering her last sow.

Sally looked at me reproachfully.

"No, 'er's called 'Susie'. Ye're not as good fer names as ye are fer faces. Oor Tom wanted to call 'er Sarah, just plain Sarah, but I sez to 'im, 'Let's call 'er Susie, after yer mother, fer she do 'mind me of 'er.' So that's 'ow she got 'er name."

"She's a fine beast," I said admiringly.

"Aye, she is an' all, and look how slowly she's turnin' ower on her side. That's so as she'll not crush any little 'un that might be behind 'er. It must be a job to keep yer eye on fourteen on 'em at once. Some o' them

heavy soos just go down wi' a bump, and if a young 'un 'appens to be under 'em, there's just a squeak, and next time ye go in, ye tak' oot a wee body flat as a pancake, that is if t'owd soo 'asn't eaten it. But ye never find Susie doin' that."

The mother was now lying comfortably on her side, her eyes closed, save when she grunted, then she half-opened them. Around her was her big family, each one rooting with its little pink nose at its favourite teat. They pulled and tugged and nudged her with all their strength, a struggling, seething mass of shiny silk bodies, curly tails and kicking legs.

"She ain't givin' 'em any milk yet," said Sally. "I reckon she knows a stranger is aboot . . . There, noo they're gettin' it."

Susie had given one long grunt of content. Simultaneously, every little snout stopped its exertions and every little body relaxed. All that could be heard was the quick breathing of the old sow and the fierce suckings of fourteen piglets.

"Have you seen anything of Joe and Alan lately?" I asked, as we reached the kitchen.

Sally nodded. "Alan were here a day or two sin' at t' blacksmith's. Oor Tom were tellin' me as 'ow 'e'd been 'avin' summat done to t' mowin' machine, so I reckon they're well on wi' t' hay harvest by now. Are ye goin' up to t'farm?"

I nodded.

A few moments later Raq and I turned our steps up the hill which leads from the village. As I neared the farm I expected to hear the rattle of the mower, but everything was silent. Away up by the High Barn I could see a field standing in cock, so concluded that a lot of the cutting had been done. In the yard I saw the brothers having a chat.

"Ye're just in time fer the ten o'clock," said Joe, and linking his arm in mine, he led me into the big kitchen where his wife welcomed me to this second snack of the day.

"I thought you would have been cutting or turning the hay," I said. "Have you finished?"

Alan shook his head. "Not yet. We've a goodish bit to cut, but" — here he pointed towards the fields — "t'watter isn't off yet."

"Fields flooded?" I asked anxiously.

Joe smiled. "No, he means that the dew is still on t'grass, and it's no good starting to cut till it's dry."

"That throws you a bit late in the day starting, and —"

"Aye, an' Summer Time doesn't 'elp us neither," Alan broke in, "but we're not very particular aboot how long we work on a farm. If we start late, we work on while there's a bit o' light left."

Hannah was just serving the bacon and eggs at that moment and she caught the last sentence.

"That's very true," she said in her own quiet way.

I knew what she was thinking: "Women's work on a farm is never done." There are no auction sales for them every week, where they can get a change and a gossip as their men-folk do — eternal baking days and food-preparing is their lot, generally speaking.

"We have good men, though," said Joe, "and we've no grumblin' when they've to do a bit extra. Did I ever tell ye aboot one farmer that worked his men hard and onreasonably late?"

"It's a good un," said Alan laughing, and looking as though he wished that he had remembered it first.

"Well," said Joe, "this feller was a hard driver and no mistake, and one night in hay-harvest, after they had worked until dark, he —"

"They'd bin at it fer some days, remember," Alan broke in.

"He said to his men: 'Noo, lads, we'll gang yam (go home) an' 'ave some supper, an' away to bed — he's a grand feller that invented bed.' Then one o' t' lads spoke up and said: 'Aye, but 'e's a grander chap that invented dark, or there wad be nae bed at all 'ere.'"

Much to Raq's disgust I left him in the stable when we set out for the High Barn. As we climbed the hill, the rattle of the mower grew louder. It was like the sound of a machine-gun in action.

"The horses are pulling well. They seem to step out better than when ploughing," I said.

"That's what I allus think," said Joe approvingly, "I rather fancy that the horses like the . . ."

"Rhythm," put in Alan rather pleased with himself. "Aye," he continued, "I fancy t' horses like the rhythm of t' mower — it's a sort o' band that makes 'em march."

Suddenly the horses stopped. I had seen Bob almost draw them back on to their haunches, so suddenly had he put on the brake and the reins. Almost simultaneously a brown bird flew out from near the cutter — it looked, from where I stood, as though it had crept out from under the machine. As it took to flight Alan said, with real pity:

"Poor little bird, it's got caught in t' cutter — one leg's gone an' all." As we reached the machine Bob said, "I niver seed that partridge till I were on top on 'er, an' it were too late to save 'er. One leg's off, but I reckon she'll live all reet — t'other un weren't touched. She were sittin' that tight on 'er nest —"

Joe was down on his knees, showing me the nest with its olive eggs, destroyed. "She would 'ave 'atched 'em oot in a couple o' days, too — what a pity."

As the mower rattled on with its merciless teeth, Alan, pointing to the nest, said:

"See, the cutter must a'most 'ave touched 'er the last time it went roond the field, but she sat on."

I tried to enter into the mind of the partridge. Did she feel at all apprehensive when she heard the men and horses come into the field? If so, Nature told her what to do. "Your best defence is to lie perfectly still." So, with fear, which increased as she heard the alarming chatter of the teeth coming nearer to her, she sat on. Why not? In a score of other instances she had proved its wisdom. When hawks were flying low, or when a fox was stalking abroad, had she not found that immobility was her security? So, with beating heart and indomitable courage, she had watched the scythe of death gradually approach what, to her, was more than her own life. Not till those gleaming teeth touched her breast feathers had she thought of herself. Then it was too late!

I left them to get on with their work. But before turning downhill, I took a long look at what to me is one of the fairest spots on earth. Below in the valley were the quiet homesteads, their blue smoke going straight up to a bluer sky. Between them and the hills was the river, gliding like a silver snake in Eden. Then I was conscious of the fragrance of newly-mown clover; the smell of the cows fresh from the pasture; the scent of bean blossom swaying in a light breeze, honeysuckle scent in heavy gusts coming through a gap in the hedge. Nature's gifts these, all of them intoxicating, and lurking somewhere in them lies truth, elusive yet enticing. But the perfume of newly-mown grass is a thing by itself — like the box of spikenard, it has to be broken before its fragrance fills the house.

CHAPTER
FOUR

Moulting Time

Passing a field we heard the sound of shouting, and looking over the gate we saw that some of the village lads were beginning their football season. I recognized

Jimmy Stordy, which reminded me that I meant to call at his mother's cottage.

When we reached the village Raq must have known that I was bound for Sally Stordy's, for he scuttled as fast as his legs would carry him ahead of me. Finding her door closed, I saw him scratch it and look up expectantly.

He had not long to wait, and as Sally stooped to pet him she looked up the street and waved me a welcome. Many others as I walked past their windows gave me a welcome too — just a nod and a pleasant smile.

"I were wond'rin' when I should be seein' ye agin," said Sally, as I took possession of her high-backed arm-chair. "I 'eard ye was on yer 'oliday. I can't kill t' fatted calf, but I can give ye a bit o' summat ye likes."

"Blackberry plate-cake?" I asked expectantly.

Sally nodded, and set one before me through which the purple juice looked rich and appetizing.

"That'll mak' it slip doon easy," she said, placing a jug of cream by it.

"It goes down easily enough without that, Sally. The flavour is excellent."

"That's 'cos t' berries 'ave 'ad a bit o' sun this year. It turns the watter in 'em into wine."

And so, while Raq enjoyed a bone on the rug in front of the fire, Sally chatted on, bringing me up-to-date with the news of the village.

"Ye 'member owd Tom Shaw, him as lived at top o' t' village, well, we buried 'im a fortnight come Monday. 'E come 'ome from work, sat doon i' 'is chair by t' fireside, an' were gone. O' course it were a shock fer Lucy, but I reckon she'll be better off wi'oot 'im. 'E'll be missed most at t' 'Black Bull'. I mind 'im when 'e were wed — 'e were a reet well set up young feller i' them days. I went to have a chat wi' 'er a week sin', and she were twinin' on' aboot t' funeral. 'Fancy,' sez she, 'a funeral, and nobbuddy there. There'd only 'ave been me and Tom's brother and sister if I 'adn't got Emma and Tom Braisby to mak' up t' party. It were sic a dead and alive affair, as ye niver did see.' 'Well, Lucy,' I sez to 'er, 'Ye should 'ave put it off till the Tuesda'. Ye see it were t' day o' Mothers' Meetin' outin' to Morecambe.

That's why nobbuddy were in t' village.' Sally sighed. "That's t' worst o' livin' in a village — nowt excitin'-like 'appens fer months, and then there comes a buryin' and an outin' on t' same day. Howsomever," here she became her old cheerful self, "ye'll be glad to 'ear Tom Carruthers and Jinnie Long's got fixed up at last. They're to be wed i' October — an' it's time they were an' all, fer they've bin walkin' oot fer eighteen 'ears to my knowledge. If I'd 'ave bin 'er I'd 'ave sent 'im aboot 'is business long sin, but some girls 'as no pride."

"You'll be sending me about my business if I don't get a move on," I said rising, for I saw there was more to come, and the September sunshine was calling.

"Ye're allus welcome," she said simply.

After leaving Sally, Raq and I set out for a point on the road where I thought I might intercept Ned with his letters. We cut across the fields, and came across him just before he went up the lane to Whiterigg.

"So ye're back agin, are ye?" was his greeting, and without another word being spoken we fell into stride. How different had been Sally's welcome. She had bubbled over with hospitality. Ned's was the welcome of acceptance. We simply took up the severed ends of comradeship, as though there had never been a break.

"D'ye see much diff'rence in t' countryside?" asked Ned.

"Yes and no. The green of the trees and hedges is not so vivid, and the hedge-bottoms look more tousled.

They've lost the spruce look of the earlier months. And of course, the hay has gone into stack, and into the Dutch barns. But there isn't much Autumn colour on the trees yet."

"I reckon ye've 'ad a free and easy kind o' holiday i' that camp o' yourn, didn't ye?"

I nodded. "We just did what we liked — wore any old thing, and threw off all the routine of city life."

"That's just what them plants is doin'. Look at them seeds on yon foxglove. Everythin' that grows as bin workin' until now — grasses, trees, shrubs — they've put oot every bit of energy they've 'ad to perfect their fruit. They've guarded 'emsels from enemies, an' grown spikes an' hairs to protect theirsels. Each on 'em 'as tried to beat 'is neighbour in gettin' more than 'is share o' sunlight an' rain — they've 'ad no rest since their green shoots appeared in t' Spring — and now they've done their work an' are 'avin' their 'oliday an' all."

He opened the gate which led to Whiterigg, and the dog and I waited for him. His words made me look round at all growing things, and I saw that what he had said was true. The plants were lounging. They cared not what they looked like. Very few gay petals now blazed their coloured blandishments to the passing insect. Their work was done — the meadowsweet and the parsleys, the yarrows, and the agrimonies were lolling in a well-earned holiday.

★ ★ ★

We walked down towards the bridge. In the lane the dog flushed two birds from the undergrowth, the one a blackbird, the other a sparrow.

"Them looks the worse for wear," was Ned's comment.

The blackbird had lost all his sleek Spring appearance, and the sunlight of his bill was dimmed. He was minus a tail feather or two, and looked slovenly, as though he could do with some grate polish shine.

The sparrow had lost his tail completely, yet he flew far better than the bigger bird. His loss of tail did not seem to incommode him very much. In plumage he, too, had lost his smartness. His browns were muddy, and his blacks, dirty greys.

"Both in the moult," I said to Ned.

He nodded, "An' it's a tryin' time for t' birds an' all."

"You mean that the dropping of their feathers makes it difficult for them to fly?"

"Aye, it's sartainly no 'elp, but it's the drain o' strength that I'm thinkin' on. There must be thousands o' feathers on a bird, and every one on 'em 'as to be replaced. Moultin' time is a testin' time. It comes when they're all tired-like after feedin' broods o' youngsters. 'Undreds of 'em never come through it alive, poor things."

Thinking of the blackbird, I said, "I noticed that he still had some of his tail feathers. I suppose they don't all fall out at once?"

"No, it's a gradual thing, except wi' some birds."

Ned did not volunteer any more information. We walked along together by the edge of the stream and watched Raq chasing the water-hens.

Suddenly amongst the reeds I saw something move, and was on the point of sending Raq to investigate when Ned motioned to me to hold him back.

"It's a mallard drake. Just squat doon here behind this bush a minute. We might get a look at 'im, and then ye'll see why I don't want t' dog to be loosed at 'im."

We waited without seeing anything for a moment or two, and then, across a small patch of open water we saw the bird make for the covering of a bigger clump of rushes.

"A duck, not a drake," I said, for I had been expecting to see a neck as green and as shiny as new laurel leaves, with a bloom of peacock blue on it, but this was just a drab brown.

Ned smiled, "That's an easy mistake to make. Ye know 'ow the drake goes into 'eclipse,' as they call it?"

I nodded. "But I only thought that meant that he lost all his flight feathers and so became practically defenceless."

"He loses everythin', and t' funny thing is that at this time o' t' year any one might, even as ye did, tak' 'im for the duck. All them wing feathers drop oot at once, and 'e skulks in t' reeds till 'e's fit to appear in comp'ny agin."

"Perhaps it's a mercy that he does lose his burnished neck and conspicuous white stripes, if he is as defenceless as you say. Their brightness would call unwanted attention to himself."

Ned agreed. "Nature does nowt by chance — the wind is allus tempered to t' shorn lamb."

Soon after we went our separate ways — Ned with his remaining letters and Raq and I to our pottering about — "doin' nowt and doin' it well," as Sally once said.

"There's no hurry, old man," I said to the dog as we lolled on a hedgebank, "we'll sit here a while."

So we watched the young robins trying to look like young fly-catchers, not a bit like their ruddy parents. We listened to the swallows chittering on the telegraph wires, and realized that they would soon start on their long trek southwards. I laughed aloud when a half-grown hare came through a gate, and for a moment stared at us, not knowing what to do. He was a strange sight with his long ears and staring eyes. Then he whisked round and showed his paces, whilst Raq, with my grip on his collar, strained and squirmed to be after him.

When the sun went down it left behind it amber and green, the trees on the hills massing themselves in great grey shadows, the quietness intensified by the bleat of some lonesome lamb, and the note of a querulous lapwing. Ah! yes, the country for me!

CHAPTER
FIVE

The Pine Wood

There is a time in Summer when one is conscious that the Spring lushness is a thing of the past — a time when, after a few days of drought, the leaves of the trees grow sombre and speak of middle-age.

But there is a time, too, in Autumn, when Spring seems to return — it is the time when the pine wood puts forth vivid emerald shoots, which shiver like delicate tassels at the end of the dark branches. Such a day it was when the dog and I wandered through a wood. Oak and elm, birch and sycamore, spoke of waning life, but the pine-tree had kept Spring-time hidden in her heart to gladden us when Autumn should touch everything else with sleepy fingers.

No wood is quite like a pine wood — with its carpet of pine-needles, dark brown, save where a stray sunbeam fires its brown into copper. Overhead the dark green canopy of leaves sway with majestic rhythm, sensitive to the slightest breath of the south wind, yet too proud to stoop even before the onslaught of the savage "north-easter." I can see the young saplings, self-sown, standing beyond the edge of the wood, the ling and heather at their base claiming the territory which the young pines had intended to make their own. In the wood itself the heather has had its day — the tall giants have starved it of sunshine, and it simply is not.

Here and there patches of bracken, straining up to catch the sun, look like graceful crinolines round the tree trunks, but other vegetation only gleams in small oases — the rest is brownness.

In some woods I allow Raq to race about as he will, but in a pine wood I feel it to be sacrilege, and keep him "to heel". There always seems a hushed awesomeness and an aromatic breath pervading all things. The tall trees arch over the long rides and the golden glory of the sun at the end of each shadowed aisle glows and shimmers.

"I thowt ye'd be roond afore long," was Jerry's greeting as he met us. "I heerd as 'ow ye'd bin at Sally's — ladies fust, o' course," he added with a sly wink. "An' what 'ave ye got there?"

I held up a dead hedgehog. Raq sniffed at it very gingerly as I held it in my fingers.

"I found it lying just outside the pine wood."

"There ain't much use carryin' it aboot wi' ye. Are ye takin' it 'ome to keep as a pet?"

I put the ball of spines on the ground and uncurled it.

"Why," said Jerry in surprise, "it's 'oller. Its inside 'as bin cleaned oot so neatly that I thowt it were a live 'un."

I smiled with quiet satisfaction at his surprise. "Yes, that is why I brought it to show you. I don't make a habit of carrying live hedgehogs about, you know."

Jerry knelt down and gave the empty carcase a minute examination.

"It's bin scooped oot inside as clean as an orange. Even the head and t' legs 'ave bin eaten an' —"

"But what did it?" I broke in. "Is it the work of a fox?"

Jerry shook his head slowly.

"Mebbe, o' course, fer I've known foxes to kill 'em. Where did ye find it?"

I described the spot. "Let's go back and 'ave a look where 'e were lying. Summat might give us a clue."

So we turned our steps towards the pine wood again.

A few minutes' tramping brought us there. Pointing to a few holes in the ground, Jerry said, "Ye can see what yon 'edgehog's been after. 'E's bin diggin' fer grubs and

beetles. 'E can't go very deep, but them claws of 'is is useful fer gettin' doon below t' surface."

"That's where he's an ally and not a foe of the farmer," said I, ever ready to make a brief out for a hedgehog.

Jerry nodded, and for a moment stopped in his examination of the ground.

"But ye'd better not mention eggs if ye're defendin' 'im. Owd Graham, o' Whiterigg yonder, 'ad a hen sittin' in an oothouse on thirteen this Spring. One night 'e 'eerd 'er cacklin' and makin' a fine carry-on. When 'e went oot to see what was t' matter, 'e found an owd 'edgehog 'avin' a' 'igh owd time wi' 'em. There was six on 'em gone afore 'e got there, and 'e'd 'ave bagged t' lot if Graham 'adn't stopped 'is little game."

"And what did he do?"

Jerry laughed. "Kicked it oot and sent it flyin' into t' duckpond."

"And did the poor beast drown?"

"Not a bit on't." laughed Jerry. "It simply swam oot, and t' next night it cam' back, and ate up t' rest of th' eggs. Ye should 'ave 'eerd owd Graham's tale o' woe. Ye'd 'ave thowt 'e'd lost a prize beast. But it sarved 'im right fer not lockin' 'is broody 'en up safe. But that don't git us any nearer to what killed this 'un."

Whilst he cast round to find any clues I gathered together a few fragments lying about. The jaws, with the gleaming white teeth, still lay on the ground. Almost every vestige of red flesh had been licked off.

A shout from Jerry interrupted me. On the soft clayey ground leading to the hedge he had found the deep claw marks of a badger.

"That's the culprit, an' a neat job 'e's made of it an' all. The inside might 'ave been scooped out wi' a spoon."

I could see what had happened — the hedgehog hunting for his small game, the badger shuffling along, not thinking of flesh food, but suddenly getting a whiff of the hedgehog's strong scent — oh, joy! a change of diet for him!

As for the hedgehog, his keen ears had caught the sound of the badger's noisy progress, and he had quickly rolled up for safety. But no spiny defence could resist the strength of paws that could burrow into hard earth as though it were yielding sand. With his two front paws the badger had by sheer strength uncurled him, and then the rest had been easy.

I showed Jerry the jaws.

"D'ye notice 'ow every tooth, both top an' bottom, is pointed and sharp? That tells ye that 'edgehogs were never made to live on grass and sich-like. 'E's a flesh-eater."

He handed me the spiny shell.

"I reckon it's your job to bury what's left on 'im 'earth to earth, and ashes to ashes' — ye know."

I am always fascinated by sights such as these, and yet they sadden me. They seem so out of place amid the serene beauty around.

Whilst the hedgehog was meeting his doom, the cool silver moonlight would be touching the bracken with evening calm, and the pines would be wafting an incense that speaks of a fairer world than we know.

"I wonder," said I, "which is real Nature — this," here I pointed to the gory spot — "or this," and my arm swept the purple hills and the sky flecked with feathery plumes of white cloud.

Jerry swung himself on to the top of a stone wall, and as he lit his pipe, said: "Both on 'em, I reckon. When ye 'ear folks talk o' t' cruelty o' Natur', it gin'rally means that they just fix both eyes on one side on't. O' course, I know all aboot that side, and it ain't a pretty thing to think aboot, but then ye must look at t' other side an' all. Would ye rather live in a world where sudden death were the gin'ral order o' things, or where ye saw thousands dyin' o' slow starvation?"

"Well," I said slowly, "I don't like the prospect of either; but if it were a case of choosing, I should prefer sudden death."

"Aye, and most folks would who 'ad a pennorth o' sense. Tak' the case o' the 'edgehog as I figures it oot i' my own mind. Thousands on 'em must be born i' this district alone every year, every one on 'em hungry and all lookin' fer t' same kind o' food. Where are they all goin' to get it from? Us folks 'ave the sense to grow the stuff we need to feed on. If we want corn we can sow it; if we want bacon we can git more pigs. But 'edgehogs can't keep breedin' pens o' slugs and beetles; the —"
Here he paused a moment.

"The demand does not govern the supply," I said.

"That's it noo, and if all on 'em lived, there'd soon be a famine in t' 'edgehog world. An', mind ye, there is millions of other critturs searchin' fer the same kind o' food. I reckon it's better to die sudden in full 'ealth than to linger on 'ungry an' weak."

"Well, that's one way of looking at things," I said, "though it is not exactly satisfying."

"One way o' lookin' at things never is," he replied.

CHAPTER
SIX

Unseen Sowers

The September sun was shining brightly as the dog and I turned our steps towards the open country. It was warm, and the Autumn sunshine was doing its best to make one believe that Summer was still with us, and that the calendar could not be relied on.

But the swallows and the house-martins were telling another tale. No longer were they busy catching insects every second of daylight. Many of them had now time to loiter; life was not so strenuous as it had been. On the roofs of barns and on telegraph wires I saw whole communities of them basking in the sunlight, preening their feathers, and generally tittivating themselves up, now that urgent family cares were past.

True, some of them were as busy as ever, for in certain nests there were still young to be fed, and as I passed underneath I could see small black and white heads peeping out of a mud doorway and calling to their parents as they flashed by, "Tweet-tweet," "Tweet-tweet."

But those on the red-tiled roofs and the balancers on the wires, were twittering and chattering as though debating some serious problem. No doubt the breeze which stirred the tops of the trees had something to do with their pow-wow, for where the sun did not penetrate it struck a little chilly. Those birds had heard, perchance, the first whisper of the north wind, and they knew that it was the signal to begin packing up their belongings.

A few more weeks will pass before we shall see the last one. In ever larger drifts the birds will pass southwards, until at last our fields will know their quick flight no more.

"Hullo," I called out to Ned as I passed his garden, "what's interesting you?"

The old postman, I could see, had been tidying up, but as I passed, he was so intent on something which lay on the ground that he never heard my approach.

"Oh, it's you, is it?" he said, greeting me with a rare smile. "I were just lookin' at this little dead thing 'ere, and I fell a wonderin'."

I entered the garden and found him looking at a dead tomtit — one which had been dead a few days and was not exactly a pretty picture to look at. I said nothing — a decomposed bird is not a thing to rhapsodize on. Ned chuckled at my prolonged silence. "It's a sign o' wisdom," he mumbled, "when ye've nowt to say, to keep yer mouth tight."

He stooped and picked up the bird, its pretty blue and saffron feathers now sadly bedraggled. It was difficult to believe that only a few days before that pitiful object had quivered with a thousand energies, and delighted the eye with a score of pretty graces.

"What has killed it?" I asked.

Ned shook his head. "Nay, that I canna tell ye. I only know that if flies 'ave any sense o' humour they'll think that they've seen a good joke when they pass by."

"It looks more of a tragedy to me," I said.

"To you, mebbe, it does," answered Ned. "But think a minute. All through its life, from the fust day its eyes oppened in the little hole in which it were hatched, it's bin chasing and livin' on flies and insecks. Niver fer a moment has it given 'em any rest. It's searched fer 'em in the bark, and up-ended itsel' to find their eggs under the leaves. It's never left no cranny in a wall wi'oot peckin' and peerin' fer their hidin' places."

He paused a moment, and by the expression on his face I knew that he expected me to make some comment. All I did say, however, was, "Yes, the tit is a life-long enemy of all flies and insects."

"That were a cautious answer," Ned said. "Howsomever, here's my point: the tomtit lives on t' flies. Now it's dead, the flies tak' their revenge, by laying their eggs in t' carcase o' their old enemy, and feasting on the very body built up by t'other flies. That's why I said just now that every fly as sees it must have a good chuckle."

"It's poetic justice," I said.

"Aye," said the postman, "them's the words I were hankerin' after."

Whilst Ned continued "doing up" his garden, I sat down on an old seat. He stowed in a corner all his vegetable rubbish, remarking that "it ud come in useful-like later on."

From over the hedge the aerial seeds of the dandelion, wisps of thistledown, silver tuftlets of willow-herb, floated. I called his attention to them.

"You'll find a few of them springing up in your plot in a few months' time," I said.

He nodded. "Aye, ye can't keep 'em oot, whatever ye do, and I don't know as I should like a garden where only the things ye put in't ever come up. It 'ud be a land o' few surprises, I reckon."

He stopped digging and rested one foot on the top of the spade's steel blade. "Did I ever tell ye 'ow I found a flower as I never knew the name on't?"

I shook my head. "It would be a rare one."

"Well," continued Ned, "I were passin' a beck up yonder. I weren't thinkin' o' anything pertickler, when all of a sudden-like I found mysen lookin' at a pale yeller flower summat like the shape o' a sweet pea. It had deep red spots and stripes on't. As soon as I set eyes on't I knew it had me beat so far as its name went. How it come there I couldn't think, but I made up me mind to try and find oot."

"Was it a foreigner?" I asked.

Ned shook his head. "I niver 'ad a chance to tak' one to anybody who could 'ave told me."

Ned turned to his digging again.

"But you haven't told me yet how it came to be by the beck," I said.

Once again the old man rested on his spade, with that pleased look which spoke of having an interested listener.

"Well," he went on, "I went up to t' beck and started lookin' around. Aboot twenty yards further up I cam' across another little clump o' the same sort."

"On the top of the bank or in the field?" I interpolated.

"On top o' t' bank owerlookin' t' beck," he answered. "So I follered by t' side o' t' watter, and every now and then I come across a few on 'em growin'. I went on and on till I got reet on top o' t' fells, where t' beck rushes oot just afront o' old Jamie Crosbie's hut."

"I've heard of him," I said. "He was the old shepherd that used to live there years ago, wasn't he? Isn't the hut in ruins?"

"Aye," said Ned. "Many's the time I've seen him when I were a little un, but he were queer and cared nowt fer us lads. But roond his cottage I found quite a goodish few of them there yeller flowers. Ye've heard 'ow fond he were o' collectin' these rare uns."

"Perhaps some migrating bird brought over a seed stuck in its feathers, or even on its feet, and it dropped off as it passed on its journey."

"It's not too onlikely," Ned said. "Howsomever, I found 'em there. I've bin up a time or two since, and there's bin no more on 'em."

Once again Ned turned to his spade. I rather fancy the old man did not care for my butting in so often, and showed it in his own way.

"But you haven't told me yet how those yellow flowers came to be growing down by Whiterigg." Then I added, "Sorry to keep interrupting."

Quite mollified, he continued, "Wind, watter, birds and animals are all seed-sowers. Ye've noticed the down of the dandelion. Do ye see that poppyhead ower yonder? Have a look at it."

I went to where he pointed, and lifted the round, drooping head. As I did so, a shower of dark seeds fell at my feet.

"Yon's a flower that waits fer t' wind to blow it from side to side. A big head on a slim stem means that the smallest o' breezes is enough to set it all of a waggle. Then, like pepper oot o' a pot, t' seed spills itsen oot. That's the way the wind 'elps. Now them yeller flowers i' Jamie's garden must 'ave blowed an' seeded. Then the beck rose wi' the rains and owerflowed its banks, mebbe. So t' seed were washed doon and bloomed where I found it."

"Perhaps," I said, "the wind blew the seeds into the beck. That would account for their dispersal too."

Ned nodded. "Aye, it might just be one way as another. What beats me is 'ow these little plants, wi'oot any brain so far as we can see, has — ev — ev —"

"Evolved," I suggested.

"That's it," he said. "Evolved a way o' gettin' their childer well placed i' life. They canna move theirsen, so they mak' use o' t' breeze and t' stream, an' birds an' animals, an' they drops 'em i' queer corners, an' so keep the earth full o' surprises."

★   ★   ★

After leaving Ned, Raq and I were passing by a wood when I heard a slight rustling. We crouched in the hedge-bottom, and I peered through. Under an oak was a fine cock-pheasant. It was some time before I could see him distinctly, for this bird, which stands out so clearly on the stubble, is hardly discernible against bracken and withering grass.

He had found a ripe acorn, but it was far too big to swallow. It was amusing to see his attempts. His bill looked like an egg-cup trying to hold an egg three sizes too large for it. Once he managed to get it somewhere

near his throat, but he had to disgorge it. Finally he picked up the treasure, and ran down the glade with it still in his bill.

"I don't think he will swallow that in a hurry," I said to Raq. "Somewhere or other he will give up the attempt, and the acorn will find a new resting-place. Perhaps an oak-tree will be the result. I wonder whether the old tree made a specially big acorn on purpose."

CHAPTER
SEVEN

The "Vet"

It was quite a refreshing experience to have a walk in the rain, and I, personally, enjoyed the heavy shower. As for Raq, he neither cares whether it rains or snows. Ordinary rain never soaks his skin; it only wets the outer layer of his coat. During a heavy shower we stood under a gaily-coloured chestnut-tree, and listened to the patter of the rain-drops, the air of which seemed to be played by the right hand, whilst the swish of the rain on the fields provided the left-hand accompaniment to the music.

I dropped in for a few moments to "Rose Bank," Alan's new home, just to see how things were progressing.

"It's a slack season for us just aboot this time o' t' year," he said; "sort o' between times. It's a bit on the early side to begin cuttin' yer turnips, and it's bin sic grand weather fer ploughin' stubble that we've well-nigh finished."

"What about your potato crop? How have they turned out?"

"Middlin'," he replied. "Plenty o' potatoes, but t' sample is small."

"Same with mine," I said, feeling that we had common ground for complaint, "I found scores and scores of small ones, and only here and there a real whopper."

"How many acres have ye, then?" he asked.

"About eight yards by ten."

"Both bein' farmers then, we can grumble together," he said with his hearty laugh.

At that moment a brisk little man entered the yard. I was told by Margaret, Alan's wife, that it was the "vet". No one who has not lived in the country can know how big a part a "vet" plays in rural life. In the town we only think of him in connexion with sick dogs. But in the country he is the guardian of all the stock. Every day he goes on his rounds, visiting patients who can neither question him nor give him any help as to what is the matter with them. All he knows is that "they are off their food," or "have a cough," and that some quick alleviation is necessary if the patient's life is to be saved. To have a full night's sleep must be a great luxury to him, for hurried news reaches him of a horse that has colic, or of some dairy cow that is in trouble with her expected calf. But what a mission in life to be able to help those whose only appeal comes through pleading, wondering eyes!

"So you've got a cow that's none too grand, have you?" asked the animal doctor.

"Aye; she's got a bit of a cough and doesn't seem herself."

45

We walked over to the building where the cow was, and the vet proceeded to examine her.

"Been lying out where there's been a bit of fog, I reckon," said he.

"That's reet. So she has. Down by t' river yonder, and it has bin a bit thick-like in the early mornin's. We're bringing oor milkers in at night now, fer it's gettin' a bit on t' cold side."

The vet nodded and looked up at the beams of the roof. On one of them hung a pulley. Without a word Alan walked over to the barn and brought back a rope.

"That'll 'od (hold) 'er, I reckon," he said, making a noose, and at the same time slipping the rope over the cow's head.

"She's got 'husk,'" Alan said, turning to me. "That's what ye're thinking, isn't it?" he said, turning to the vet.

I asked what it meant and watched the vet getting out his penknife and cleaning it. He then took a syringe out of his bag and filled it with some kind of fluid.

"Husk," explained Alan to me, "is a kind o' germ that settles on low-lyin' land — a kind o' insect that crawls on fogged grass. Cows tak' it up when they're grazin', and it sticks in their gullet and mak's 'em sick."

"It must be something like the liver-fluke which sheep eat on pastures near to rivers, I suppose."

Alan nodded. "The disease is different, o' course, but they both contract it in the same kind o' way. Now we're ready," he added, fixing the rope through the pulley and beckoning me to help. We pulled until the cow's head began to lift, and we did not slacken until the throat was stretched taut.

"She's not kicking much," I said.

"I reckon she's not got ower much breath to kick wi', wi' 'er wind-pipe hauled up like yon."

The vet ran his fingers over the stretched throat and deftly, but surely, he thrust in his knife, making a small incision in the air-shaft. Then the syringe did its work.

"I reckon that stuff'll tickle the germs up a bit," said Alan.

"She'll be all right now," said the vet stroking his patient, and taking a last look at her eyes. "It's all over, old lady," he said to the poor beast in a soothing voice.

"And how often will you have to do that to her?" I asked, as we walked to the gate to see him off.

"Oh, as a rule, one dose is sufficient," he replied.

As we stood watching the car rattling away to visit another patient, Alan said: "Wonderful man yon. Would ye ever think that he was ower eighty? He lives a'most next door, and we hear his car comin' in at all hours o' the night. He's as wick as many a man o' sixty. It's marvellous."

As the sun was now appearing through the clouds, I resisted all the wiles of Alan and his wife to make me stay and have a "bite o' summat," and Raq and I wandered out through the village towards the wide open spaces. What a relief it is for tired eyes to have an uninterrupted view of the countryside — the open mosaic of the fields — the fresh tinge of green brought up by the rain on parched land, the fresh brown of newly-ploughed earth, and here and there a stubble field still yellow, though all its golden currency now

47

stands in sturdy stacks. And behind it all the fells, with their patches of waning purple, and the outcrop of the rocks, now washed grey and clean by the showers.

Hearing the hum of a threshing-machine, I made my way to a farm which stood by the roadside. The music of the thresher is best heard from a distance. All was bustle and noise when we got near.

"Many rats about?" I asked one of the lads as he carried a sack full of oats.

"An odd un or two," he answered. "There's a few mice runnin' oot, but th' 'ens is after 'em."

We stood and watched them. Round the stack the hens certainly had congregated. Then a tiny figure darted out and sought the safety of one of the buildings. Being out of its usual "run," it did not run with its usual speed or certainty. It had almost reached safety, when it was seen by an old "Rhodie," who gave it one peck, and the little mouse lay dead.

"Do they eat the mice?" I asked, as the lad passed me.

"Some on 'em try one or two, but I 'ave 'eerd as it mak's 'em sick."

"Perhaps it's an acquired taste," and seeing him look a trifle blank, I added, "Like a taste for mushrooms, you know."

He grinned. "Mebbe 'tis."

⋆　⋆　⋆

On we walked again until a heavy shower drove me to take shelter under a big yew-tree which guarded a well-kept garden. A roadman left his tidying-up of the road-fringes and joined me as the rain fell more heavily.

"Showery," I remarked.

"Aye, but it's needed, though my job is weary work if t' rain is lashin' doon."

I turned to examine the garden with its dahlias still in bloom, and its dainty lavender and pink Michaelmas daisies still fresh. Then I saw a movement in the shadows of the shrubbery, and a moment later to my surprise, a fine cock-pheasant stalked into full view. He saw us too, but showed no sign of fear.

"There's a fine pheasant in that garden," I said to the roadman.

"Aye," he said. "It's there pretty often when t' shootin' season comes in. I reckon 'e knows t' sound of a gun as well as you and me, an' no sooner does September come along an' 'e 'ears a gunshot than ye'll find 'im somewhere i' this garden. Ye see, t' lady as lives 'ere won't 'ave birds interfered wi'. It's a sort o' —"

"Sanctuary," I said, helping him.

"Aye," he said, "nowt's ever allowed to be shot in 'ere — an' 'e knows it an' all. 'E's bin aboot noo fer a year or two. 'E's a knowin' un, I can tell ye. Watch 'im now. 'E's feedin' right in front o' th' house as saucy as ye like. Thank ye, sir, I don't mind if I do," he added as he took my proffered tobacco-pouch. As he filled his clay pipe he said with a new tone of respect, "It ain't often gen'lemen same as you smokes twist."

I laughed and thought, "Heaven forbid." I always keep a little stock of twist handy when I'm in the country. It loosens tongues, and tones down the glaring white of my collar!

CHAPTER
EIGHT

Gathering and Scattering

As Raq and I came nearer to the farm we saw a thin curl of smoke rising from an unusual part of the buildings. There rumbled on the still air the moaning drone of machinery.

"They're threshing too, Raq," I said.

Soon we saw the great machine being fed, and, along with Alan and Joe, watched for a few moments the sifter at work.

"Do you use the straw for anything but bedding?" I asked.

For answer Alan pointed to the cows which were grazing on a distant pasture.

"We shall feed them on't fer a time — chop it up fer 'em along with other stuff," he said.

"Till aboot Christmas," Joe added.

"I thought," I said, "when you brought the cattle in from the fields that you gave them hay."

"Not at first," said Alan decisively; "straw first — then hay. If ye starts 'em off on hay they'd never look at the straw."

"Keep the best wine until last," Joe said.

"Which reminds me," continued Alan, removing his cap and rubbing the top of his head as though he were massaging an indolent reminiscence, "o' th' advice an old man gave to a parson, 'Don't strike twelve to start off wi', start at one, and then ye'll leave room fer developin'.'"

"He meant," said Joe, "give yer congregations straw, chopped up fine, ye know, and then when hay comes along, it'll be mighty sweet."

"Aye, that's it, I reckon," said Alan; "but it means that ye have to have a mighty good crop o' hay. What if ye run short?"

"Keep sowin'," said Joe laconically.

I was going to ask them about the sowing of oats and clover and "the rotation of crops," when I noticed Raq bound forward and welcome a newcomer. As it was Ned with a handful of letters, I felt the time was not opportune, so I left them to their work, and set off with the postman on his round.

"Interestin' place that stack-yard," said Ned to me, by way of opening up a conversation.

"Storing time," I murmured.

The postman nodded. "Ever think," he asked, "what a wunnerful thing it is that the two things most necessary to human life can be stored up easily — corn and water? All ye needs is a dry place and a tank, and ye can hoard 'em up fer years, and they're there when ye want 'em."

"I hadn't thought of that," I said, beginning to turn over the suggestion in my mind. Fruit? No, that would not keep indefinitely. Meat? Vegetables? None of them were so easily preserved.

On the still autumn air there floated down to us a cry that distills in its metallic call the essence of solitude and wildness — "Honk! Honk!" My companion caught hold of my arm and pointed to a moving V of birds that winged their way westwards.

"Wild geese," he said. "They've come from the Arctic snows to winter here on the stubbles and on the estuaries." He paused a moment whilst we watched them — necks outstretched, legs straight out underneath their tails, and wings which cut the air with a whistle.

"They have to foller their food," he said, "and that mak's 'em wanderers with no abidin' place. We stores ours up and settles down in one place. Migration," he added, "is just another name fer 'food-follerin'.'"

I was about to ask him a few questions on this subject, but on looking up saw that the old man was absorbed with his own thoughts.

"Two things," he said suddenly, "are goin' on at this time o' the year — a scatterin' and a gatherin'. Most folk thinks that Autumn is the layin'-up time; not many thinks on't as a layin'-oot season as well."

He turned aside into some bushes which lined a wood, and returned with a few hazel-nuts and empty shells in his hand. Showing the ripe nuts, he handed me the remnants, saying, "What's cleaned 'em oot?"

I examined them critically, and then said, "Squirrels."

He nodded and said, "Aye, but which is the squirrels' work and which isn't?"

Some of the shells were almost intact, save that a small hole had been drilled at the top, and through this the kernel had been deftly extracted.

"Wood-mouse," said Ned, as I looked inquiringly at him.

I held up another and looked at it attentively. The bottom end had been bitten irregularly, carelessly.

"Squirrel work," said Ned. "Everything he does, he does i' jerks. Ye can see it i' the way he bites oppen them shells."

"And what about this one?" I said, showing him a shell that had been bitten more methodically, and in more leisurely fashion.

"Dormouse," Ned explained, and I could imagine its little hand-like paws, gripping the nut. "Squirrels, as ye know," he said, "are gatherers at this time o' the year. They finds oot little cupboards and hides in 'em the Winter store. All sorts o' places they use. Sometimes they comes across a nut and runs off to a bare patch o' ground and scrats it in."

"The marvel to me is how they remember where they put things," I said.

"They don't," said Ned, with a smile. "They fergits half of 'em, and that's where the hazel bushes begins to chuckle. Look at them clusters o' nuts," he said, pointing to the hedge. "Every one on 'em is a bush in em — em —"

"Embryo," I said, finding the word for which he hunted — a word which he had stored in his mind's cupboard but could not recall.

"That bush knows that scores of its seeds'll be eaten. Knows, too, that many on 'em'll be stowed away. It wants 'em buried. It can't go and plant 'em itself, 'cos it's rooted tight i' the ground. So t' squirrel steps in, eats some, buries t'others, fergits all aboot most on 'em, and then Mother Earth does the rest. Up comes the tiny sprouts i' the Spring, and bare patches become

covered wi' swayin' hazel-twigs."

"Do you mean to tell me that the hazel-bush schemes like that?" I asked sceptically.

"Why shouldn't it?" said Ned. "It's alive. Why does it make so many nuts? Because," he said, answering his own question, "it knows that only a few will ever have a chance o' growin' up."

He paused for a moment to consider how he should best put his points.

"Look around ye," he said. "What's the meanin' o' such a harvest o' seeds? Everywhere ye turns bushes, grasses, plants, turnin' 'em oot by the million. It's because they know the terrible risks which every seed has to face. They know that some'll be eaten, others fall on stony ground, some be blown into the river and perish. Natur' allus leaves a margin for life's mischances."

Ned left me for a few moments whilst he delivered his letters to a cluster of cottages. When he returned I was bending over Raq, who was yelping with pain.

"What's the matter?" he inquired anxiously.

"He's in an awful mess with some sticky kind of burr," I answered. "It's entwined in his coat. I found him trying to bite them out, but he was not successful, so I'm pulling them out, and he's not enjoying it."

The old postman knelt down and helped me in my task. When it was finished he gave a quiet chuckle and held up one of the tenacious burrs.

"Look at it," he said tersely. "Tell me what you see. Look carefully with this magnifier," he added, handing to me a small pocket lens. Whilst Raq finished his toilet I scrutinized the specimen.

"It's uncommonly like a plant hedgehog," I said. "From the centre spines radiate."

"Anything else?" asked Ned. "Look at them spines."

"Every spine has a hook on it, and —"

"That'll do," said Ned. "What did the plant, the burdock, fer that's what it is —"

"Makes fine herb beer," I interpolated.

But I saw that Ned did not appreciate my interruption, so I subsided.

"Why did the burdock mak' them hooks?" he went on. "Because," he continued, "it knew there were such things as animals with woolly coats. Ye've got one clinging to yer stockin's this very minute."

I plucked it off and looked at it with renewed interest.

"The hazel-bush makes its nut sweet so that it may be snatched off fer food. It entices with an object in view, as I've just told ye. The burdock, however, tries another dodge. It gives its children barbs, clingers. It, too, wants to scatter its seeds. So when an old sheep

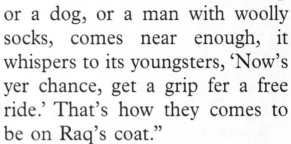

or a dog, or a man with woolly socks, comes near enough, it whispers to its youngsters, 'Now's yer chance, get a grip fer a free ride.' That's how they comes to be on Raq's coat."

I looked down at the burdock burrs scattered on the grass, and Ned continued:

"The sheep'll rub 'em out o' their wool by scrapin' themselves agin an old post or gate, an' you'll stoop down and pluck the seed off yer legs. But in any case the plant's using you as a scatterer — a sower."

On our way homewards I met some of the village lads. Jimmy Stordy was amongst them. I noticed that he had on what looked like a new pair of trousers, so evidently he had his heart's desire at last. By the look of them I judged that he had been climbing trees again, and the apple which he was munching confirmed my opinion.

As I turned the corner I saw him throw the core at one of his companions. The boy ducked, and it passed harmlessly into the hedge.

I saw the apple-tree mapping out its plan of campaign. The precious seeds were to be planted. That was its object. I saw it surrounding them in the Spring with acrid pulp, for the seeds were not mature. The unpalatable flavour was in reality a defence.

Then, in Autumn, I saw the apple painting its surface with a tempting glow. Every hue whispered to the passer-by, "Taste and see that I am good."

Jimmy had seen and tasted and had thrown away the core. I fancied that the apple-tree at that moment was congratulating itself on its sound strategy.

Squirrels and nuts, hooks and stockings, apples and mischievous boys — what strange chances replenish the face of the earth.

CHAPTER
NINE

On the Fells

"Enjoyin' it?" asked Jerry, as we tramped over the fells.

"Fine, thanks. Just the morning for a tramp," I answered, as I stopped to look at the beauty which lay below us in the valley — the undulating fields of brown and green, with a touch of chocolate in the stripped hedges. Here and there a tree was still glowing with its Autumn currency. The river, like a silver snake, glided past quiet homesteads. We watched the farmer and his men at work, and now and then busy women folk would come to the kitchen door, some shaking mats, others carrying a bucket or a brush.

Raq was thoroughly enjoying himself in the heather. After exploring a big patch which completely covered him he would leap up into the air to see where we were. He gave chase to several rabbits, but was always miles behind, for the rabbits knew their runs under the bushes, and the dog could not make much headway against barriers.

"See yon windhover?" This was Jerry's name for a kestrel hovering over a field. At times the bird was literally motionless in the air. It would then move on fifty yards or so, and once more search the ground beneath for a meal. We watched it for some time, but were never fortunate in seeing it swoop to earth.

"There's not much aboot fer 'er, seemingly," said Jerry. "She's scrattin' 'ard this mornin' fer 'er breakfast. All t' mice and voles must be lyin' a-bed late this mornin'. Keep on the low side o' these fells fer a bit," he added. "We'll climb up yon spout."

I looked ahead. On our right, hill after hill, rounded and curved by centuries of fierce rain and frost, stood sentinel over the smiling valleys. A mile away I could see the entrance to the "spout," a narrow deep ghyll scooped out of the mountain side.

"Hi!" shouted Jerry. "What's that dog o' yourn got?"

"It's too dark in colour for a rabbit," I said, as we watched Raq picking his way through the heather gullies.

A moment later, with his tail indicating his pleasure, he brought me a cock grouse.

"You bad dog," I growled. "What —"

"Hold on! Afore ye scolds 'im let's 'ave a look at t' bird. It's dead reet enough, but circumstantial evidence ain't allus what it seems."

I took the bird from the dog's mouth and handed it to Jerry. While he was examining it Raq was looking very reproachfully at me.

"'E never killed this 'un," said the poacher. "To start wi', it's not warm, so it ain't a freshly killed 'un. Feel it. It's neck's broken an' all. Yon dog would niver seize it by t' neck, would 'e? 'Ave a look yersel'."

I examined it, and being thoroughly convinced of the dog's innocence, I patted him. "Sorry, old man," I said affectionately. "I was a bit hasty in blaming you. Good dog!"

It was almost worth while being cross with him to see the response he made to the old endearing tones. There was no trace of sulking or temper. He just gave a prance, the old sparkle gleamed in his eyes, and once more he disappeared into the heather, wagging his tail.

"How did this grouse meet its end?" I asked.

"Let's walk ower yonder where t' dog found it. Mebbe we shall find oot. Pop it in yer bag. I gets plenty on 'em. Ye'll be sayin' 'Fer these an' all other mercies' ower it ter-morrer."

We walked over and examined the place carefully. On the ground were a couple of dark feathers. Pointing to a wire fence near, Jerry said, "That's done it."

"You mean that the grouse dashed against the wire?"

"Aye, early this mornin' when t' mist were on."

He glanced up and down the wire fence. "Ye'll notice as 'ow this bit o' wire is new. There's bin a gap 'ere I've noticed fer ower a twelvemonth, and birds as knows this district well flies through 'ere knowin' there's a gap. But yon poor grouse was flyin' low this mornin' 'cos of the mist. Birds is apt to keep low i' fog, ye know. He either fergot t' wire 'ad been mended or didn't know aboot it, so crashed, poor thing. Howsomever," he added with a grin, "it's an ill wind . . . You and yer missus 'll be able to grouse ter-morrer."

"It's on John Fell's land, you know," I said.

"John Fell be 'anged," said Jerry. "By the time ye've shown 'im how 'onest ye is, it'll be getting on fer dusk.

If ye'd rather leave it for t' rats, put it down, or give it me. I'll stand the chance o' t' recording angel chalkin' it up agin me."

"He'll have used up all his chalk on you already, Jerry," I said with a smile.

We pushed on through the thick undergrowth. From the cliffs a lordly peregrine dashed off at our approach, and as he passed over the lower fields we saw the small birds flying for the safety of the hedges. But the peregrine was not intent on hunting.

As we reached the entrance to the ghyll I called the dog to heel. The very majesty and stillness of the place made me stand still. The sides of the "spout" rose in lovely steep curves; their bases were covered with grass and heather, on which the small mountain sheep, looking like grey dots, browsed. Their hill-tops looked like battlements of grey rocks. From the far end a silver streak fell in cascades. It gathered its broken waters into a stream which dashed down the centre of the ghyll. A dipper, curtseying on its stone, when it saw us, flew up stream. Further on a heron rose cumbrously at our approach, and his metallic voice echoed noisily in the silence.

"What a wonderful spot, Jerry," I almost whispered. "God's own cathedral."

Jerry nodded. "In these lonely kind o' places," he said earnestly, "I almost feel religious-like."

I nodded. It was no place for words.

★   ★   ★

By the time we had climbed to the top of one of the spurs we were ready to rest. So we lit our pipes and propped our backs against one of the grey boulders. All we could hear at first was the sound of the light breeze as it rippled over the tops of the hills, not unlike the sound of the tide rolling in on the beach.

Two buzzards flew high up in the blue. They were circling with outstretched wings, and never seemed to make a wing beat. They might have been lighter-than-air machines so perfectly did they float. "I've laid on my back fer 'ours i' summer time in t' heather watching 'em sailin', till I nigh fancied I were up wi' 'em."

Raq was seated by us. He too, was tired after the heavy climb. I noticed that he kept his gaze fixed in one direction. At first I did not take much notice of it, but when he still kept looking one way I called Jerry's attention to it.

The old poacher took his cue from the dog, and after watching him for a time, said, "There's summat movin' aboot under t' crest o' yon crag o'er yonder. It's a bit in t' shadder."

"Take my field-glasses then," I said.

"It's an owd dog-fox," said Jerry. "Every 'untsman i' this district knows 'im well by sight. Leastways, they knows 'is hind parts," he added, laughing, "fer it's all they iver sees. 'Ave a good look at 'im. He's takin' an airin' under cover o' t' brow o' yon 'ill."

63

After a bit of searching about I at last focussed on him.

"He looks a grizzled old warrior. About as tough as they make them. He's dropping down the hill-side now, and seems to be making for the fields."

"He'll be makin' fer yon covert down there. The 'untsman 'as found 'im in there many a time."

"And they've never yet succeeded in getting him?" I asked.

Jerry shook his head. "'E allus leads 'em a fine dance. I've knowd 'im cover up his scent when th' 'ounds were after 'im by runnin' through a flock of sheep. Once I seen 'im do it by leapin' on t' back of an owd tup. It galloped wi' 'im reet doon t' field, and then Reynard leapt on to yon wall, and finished by paddlin' along in the beck reet up to them rocks where 'e lives."

"I suppose that by leaping on to the sheep it broke his tracks. He wouldn't leave any scent when he paddled in the stream either, would he?"

Jerry nodded. "The 'ounds were all upset. Ye could see 'em castin' roond fer t' scent. Then one on 'em got wind of 'im on t' wall, and let forth a great bayin'. That give 'em all fresh 'ope, but they were done agin as soon as they reached t' beck side."

"There he goes, Jerry. Look."

"And whilst 'ounds was tryin' to pick up his scent, that owd beggar sat ootside on them rocks as cheeky as ye like, watchin' 'em, wi' a broad grin on 'is owd mask. 'E knew reet enough that even if they found out where 'e'd gone to earth they couldn't dig 'im oot."

From up the quiet valley came the excited shrieks of angry birds.

"He's gone into that wood, Jerry. Do you hear the birds?"

"Aye, and by the noise 'e's not very welcome, neither. Them jays is cursin' 'im. They'll give 'im no peace. Look! they've chased 'im oot. See, 'e's runnin' alongside o' t' hedge, now. 'E's makin' fer t' far wood. 'E can outwit the hunt an' 'ounds, but them jays 'll tak' a deal o' shakin' off."

As he disappeared from sight silence reigned once more, and all we could hear was the occasional bleat of a sheep, and the breeze making a lyre of the serrated ridges of the rocky heights.

CHAPTER
TEN

Driven Birds

"This isn't much of a morning for a walk, old man," I said to the dog, as we faced a landscape wreathed in November mist.

Yet I was quite hopeful that it would clear up, for above the mist was white light, and I rather fancied that higher up still everything was clear. Raq, nosing about the hedges, looked thoroughly soaked to the skin, but on parting his top-coat with my fingers, I found, as usual, that his under coat was warm and dry.

Walking along a lane, I stopped beneath a tree to watch the antics of a starling. He was as merry as though the sun were shining, and clucked, gurgled, and chattered in his curious jargon as though he had a big audience to listen to him. He finished his performance by giving a perfect imitation of the plover's Spring love-call. He could not possibly have heard that wild music for many months, and yet he remembered it perfectly. What an imitator he is.

As I had hoped, the mist eventually cleared up. A pale sun lit up the landscape, touching with fire the oaks and chestnuts that still clung to some of their Autumn foliage.

By the side of an old wall covered with ivy I stood and waited for Ned. I passed the time watching the insect life which swarmed round the pale green flowers of the ivy. When we think of wild flowers we hardly ever

THE VENTRILOQUIST

think of ivy-bloom, and yet it must mean a great deal to the tiny frail insects. It is the last supply of the year of sweet nectar, and I saw bees, a wasp or two, drone-flies, and bluebottles, all greedily searching for what meant life to them.

The old postman swung down the lane with the firm tread of a vigorous younger man.

"A moist morning, Ned," I said by way of greeting.

"We can do wi' it, an' it's what we must expect this time o' t' year. If this dryness continues it'll mean a poorer Spring . . . I gave 'em a good coatin' o' dubbin afore I come out," he added, looking down at his boots.

I made a mental note to dubbin mine too when I got home.

Ned pointed to the stream, which I could see glistening amongst the alders. "There's not much water aboot yet ye see; t' beck's just aboot average."

I didn't see quite what he was driving at.

"Do you mean that there hasn't been enough rain yet to fill the wells?"

"Aye, that's reet enough; but unless we gits rain an' wet mist this time o' t' year, t' land doesn't git what it needs fer makkin' greenery i' t' Spring. I mean all these leaves lyin' aboot — millions an' millions on 'em. The land needs 'em all. The rain and mist dissolves 'em, rots 'em, and t' dust o' their leaves becomes the land's Autumn tonic. It's Natur's way o' fertilizin'."

"That's what gardeners call leaf-mould, I suppose."

He nodded. "That's it noo, an' it's the cradle o' millions o' seeds."

"And what about the beck?"

Ned did not reply, but as we crossed over a small brook that flowed into the beck, he pointed out the high-water mark.

"Look around while I tak' these letters to t' farm up yonder, an' ye'll see what I mean."

So I poked about amongst the sodden leaves, left by the beck as it subsided, and I was amazed at the variety of flotsam and jetsam I was able to gather on the bank side — beech mast, chestnuts, burdock burrs, rat's tail, and seeds of every kind of grass.

"Well?" Ned asked as he returned.

I showed him a handful.

"Now ye see what I mean. If yon small brook carries doon so much, what will the rivers and the bigger streams do? An' when the rivers flood and cover t' land, ye can see what they leaves behind. T' rivers and becks is one o' Natur's biggest seed-sowers. That's why I allus likes a flood or two at t' back end o' t' year."

As we walked on I told Ned about the insects I had been watching.

"Aye, just now, when there's a bit o' ivy blossom aboot, all t' bees bestir theirsel's, an' some days they looks as busy as i' Summer. They carries on as if it were their last chance o' takkin' in Winter stores. I can show ye better what I mean if we could find some ivy."

So we walked on until we came to a thick clump that clung round an old outbuilding. Numerous bees were to be seen busy foraging around.

"Them's new 'ands at the game," said Ned. "They've niver known the days when t' flowers were ower-stocked wi' pollen an' nectar. Only born, mebbe, a few weeks sin'. They're Winter bees."

"And where are the old ones which searched the clover and the lime blossom?"

"Oh, they're dead. Some on 'em would only live about six weeks, and then die, worn out. These'll live longer so far as time goes, but it'll not be such an' excitin' busy life fer 'em. They'll 'ave to face the cold, and, mebbe, the scarcity o' Winter. They'll just live on long enough to be the nurses o' the first babies i' Spring. If they're lucky they may feel t' sun in March as they go into t' fields, but they'll niver know the joy o' Summer when t' hive's hummin' wi' excitement bringin' in big cargoes from t' fields. Poor lil' beggars! They are hatched oot just to be drudges. Winter bees, that's what they is."

As we got near the end of Ned's round, Raq became very fussy and excited. I wondered what was upsetting him until we turned a corner and saw three sportsmen taking up their stand outside a wood. Raq had heard the guns in the distance.

"John Fell's got a shoot on to-day," I said.

"Would ye like to wait a bit and watch 'em?"

I shook my head, "I'm not fond of seeing the birds shot, Ned. Besides, I might annoy them if I cheered when a bird managed to escape."

Ned chuckled. "I didn't think ye'd enjoy t' shooting, but when t' beaters gits to work in t' woods, it's interestin' to see t' birds comin' oot fer safety."

"I never thought of that. Yes, let's stand in the corner of that hedge. I'll keep the dog to heel. He's had a good hunt all day, though he hasn't found very many rabbits 'sitting out.'"

"It's a bit too damp like," was Ned's comment.

From where we stood we soon had a splendid view of the end of the wood, where it opened out on the stubble. Soon we could hear the tap-tap of the beaters' sticks as they rather noisily waded through the undergrowth and tapped the trees as they passed.

We heard the usual protest and alarm of the blackbirds, as they reached the wood-end and scattered right and left to the hedges. Then I saw a couple of birds fly noisily out of the wood. By the flash of blue on their wings I knew that they were jays.

"They knows a thing or two," said Ned. "They're not goin' to the end where the 'guns' is standin' waitin'. See 'em? They've come to t' side of t' wood. Watch! They'll fly reet ower us. Trust them to know where safety lies."

There was only one shooter on their side of the wood, and it was amusing to notice how well the jays judged their way of escape — well out of range of his left barrel.

Then the smaller birds began to appear. The robins did not seem very flustered, but the chaffinches and tits of all kinds seemed to have entirely lost their sense of direction. A tawny owl flew out, and this caused extra panic amongst the small birds, and many of them turned back, preferring the risk of facing the beaters.

The "gun" nearest to us was so busy watching the owl that he did not notice a lovely bird, with plumage as brown as a beech leaf, fly out, and so was too late to pull the trigger. It flew softly with zigzag flight.

"Woodcock," said Ned, with evident pleasure that he had got away safely.

Then the pheasants began to appear, and the guns began. A whirr of wings, a loud report, a sudden sinking of a proud head, a sagging of wings, and then the plop of a poor limp body on the ground.

One bird dropped, and immediately started to run away.

"Wing broken," said Ned, and before I could stop Raq, he was off like a shot after it. Right down the bottom of the hedge went the pheasant, and I could see the sedges swaying, as the dog pushed them aside in his impetuous dash. On through the hedge at the bottom of the field they went. We lost sight of them, so I started after him, as I preferred him safely by my side with so many guns about.

"It's not much use yer goin'. Yon bird may run fer miles."

So we waited until the beaters appeared at the edge of the wood. Then, looking down the field, we saw Raq jump through the hedge carrying the pheasant in his jaws. Triumph was written in his every movement.

In full view of the shooters he brought it to my feet. It was still alive, and I could not bear to see the scared look in its eyes, so handed it to Ned, who, with a dexterous twist, put it out of its misery.

"There ye are," he said, holding open a wing, and I saw that it was slightly splintered.

Calling to one of the shooters, he held the bird aloft and cried, "Here's yer victim. I'll leave it 'ere fer ye."

Then, with Raq at our heels, we left them to it.

CHAPTER ELEVEN

Keen Sight

When Raq and I reached the open country we found it veiled in a mist that was almost white fog. A sharp nip was in the air, and as the warmer vapours rose from the earth so were they condensed into whiteness. As the moisture gathered on the branches, I could hear the drip-drip of the water on the fallen leaves — one of Nature's methods of dissolving them, so that whatever treasure they possess may sink once again into Mother Earth.

The smaller birds seemed bewildered by the mist, and dared not venture from the thickets and hedges. The rooks, however, were of a bolder mind, and, as I stood, a small contingent left their roosting-place and flew a few yards over my head. The wood-pigeons I could hear in the wood. Even hunger could not tempt them from the security of their perches.

Raq was disgruntled, for he could find nothing. It was a day neither for sight nor scent, and his favourite hunting-places were in mist. Pheasants did not seem to find it so very troublesome, for several of them stalked abroad. As they usually walk when in search of food, they could take their time in leisurely fashion. As a rule a pheasant, when hungry, never flies to any fancied place — he stalks there with complacent mien and unhurried steps. He reserves his wings for lifting him out of danger, and for returning to the safety of the woods.

We sought out John Fell's cottage, and as I climbed upwards I could see that the mist was more in the valley than anywhere else. In fact, where the trees stood on rising ground their tops were in clear light, whilst their bases were still shrouded.

John was busy cleaning his steel traps when we arrived, and by the time he had scraped away the clay, and judiciously given them a drop of oil, the morning was clearing.

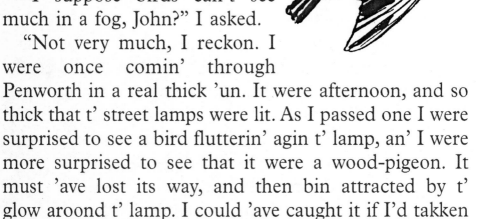

"I suppose birds can't see much in a fog, John?" I asked.

"Not very much, I reckon. I were once comin' through Penworth in a real thick 'un. It were afternoon, and so thick that t' street lamps were lit. As I passed one I were surprised to see a bird flutterin' agin t' lamp, an' I were more surprised to see that it were a wood-pigeon. It must 'ave lost its way, and then bin attracted by t' glow aroond t' lamp. I could 'ave caught it if I'd takken the trouble to climb up, I reckon. I've summat to show ye."

He got up and went towards the cottage, leaving me in the outhouse, and in a minute or two returned with a newspaper.

74

"I saved this, thinkin' I should see ye afore long," he said. "I thowt it would int'rest ye, seein' as 'ow ye're allus fiddlin' aboot wi' a camera."

The picture he pointed to was a photograph of the Isle of Man actually taken from the top of one of the Cumberland hills.

"It says summat aboot bein' took wi' a new sort o' plate. I reckon it's wonderful, fer it's sixty miles mebbe from t' Isle o' Man. An' d'ye see 'ow nearly every tree comes oot as clear as daylight? Ye can a'most see t' birds flittin' aboot — sixty miles!" he added. "'Ave ye ever seen one like it? They'll be takkin t' man in t' moon 'avin' his dinner next, I reckon."

Laughing, I explained to him as best I could how there were certain rays of light called infrared rays, invisible to our eyes, and yet which could, under certain conditions, get through the lens to the sensitive plate of a camera. "If our eyes were more sensitive, John, we could use the same rays, and the probability is that we should be able to see quite clearly through fog."

John picked up the paper and gazed at it again. "It reminds me o' summat that I seed a few years sin. A pal o' mine were fair mad on keepin' foreign birds, and t' colours o' them birds were a sight to see. We was watchin' one as it were flyin' up, his throat full-oot an' singin' like a thrush. The notes went up and up, a step at a time, just like a 'roller' canary. Then we thowt it had finished singing, for we couldn't 'ear nowt — but would ye credit it, *its throat were out as full as ever,* and its 'ead were still turnin' from side to side."

"Do you mean that it was still singing, but that you couldn't hear it?"

"That's just it, and when I come to figur' it oot," here John pointed wisely with his forefinger to his temple, "I cam' to t' conclusion that yon bird's notes were too 'igh fer our 'earing to catch."

"That's interesting, John, but what has it to do with what we were talking about?"

"Everythin'. Just as our eyes ain't sensitive, so our ears ain't neither."

"We are not tuned in, I suppose," I hazarded, but as he did not seem to catch my meaning, I let it pass.

He sat staring at the photo in silence for some time, now and then giving a quiet "humph." Then he gazed at the hills, which were just becoming visible, and I knew he was working out some problem.

"What's bothering you?" I asked at length.

"I were just wonderin' whether I'd found oot at last summat that's puzzled me fer years. Ye know 'ow a kestrel hovers ower t' land. I've pointed it oot a time or two to ye. An' ye know 'ow it can swoop doon an' pick up a small mouse or even a beetle?"

I nodded, though I could not see what he was driving at.

"Well, 'as it ever struck ye as queer that a bird aboot a 'underd feet up can see summat so small when it's lyin' in t' grass? What special sort of eyes 'as it got, think ye?"

I looked at the picture with new interest, and as I looked up, he caught my eye and nodded his head approvingly.

76

"Aye," said he, with a smile, "ye're on t' scent. Leastways, ye're on the track o' what I'm thinkin'."

"You are inclined to think, John, that, just as that foreign bird's mate could hear it singing long after your ears had failed to catch it, so the kestrel's eyes may be more sensitive than ours, and he may be able to use the light rays better than we can, and so see the smallest objects."

"There's no tellin'," he answered laconically. "An' there's another fellow that don't need 'specks' on, neither. Ye mind them barn owls as used to be up at t' High Barn. At nights, just as dusk came on, one on 'em used to come oot and sit on an owd bare branch. Ye could see 'im twistin' round 'is 'ead as though it were fitted on a swivel, an' 'is body still as a stone. Then he'd suddenly pounce doon on to t' grass ower twenty yards away, an' ye'd 'ear 'is 'ooked bill crack some lil' beggar's skull. 'Ow does 'e see that mouse movin' in t' shadders twenty yards away?"

"But don't forget the size of his big eyes, John. They're like the big end of my binoculars. They must let in a lot of light."

"I ain't fergettin' that, but I'm just wondrin' agin whether the eyes o' that barn owl uses t' same ray o' light as that camera ye were tellin' me of."

"A jolly good guess, John. You've given me lots to think about. This photographic discovery may answer all our questions."

Being nearly dinner-time I left John, as he had to do a few odd jobs.

As Raq and I passed into the open fields the sun peeped out for a few moments, and the hedgerows, which had seemed so lifeless, began to show movement. Birds peeped out from their sheltering places, and their first concern seemed to be their toilet. Mounted on the tops of the branches, how meticulously they preened their outer sodden plumage, whilst their downy feathers underneath were all passed through their bills, which acted as a comb. How particular they were to look well-groomed.

Whilst Raq was nosing amongst the grassy tufts and finding nothing, I stopped to watch the rooks sallying forth to their feeding grounds, when suddenly I heard a sound which I had heard on one of my last walks with 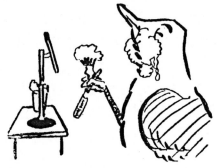 Ned. It was the "Honk" of wild geese. Right over my head they passed, and there must have been a couple of hundred of them. They were flying high, and their heads were turned seawards. I could hear the sharp staccato call, which seemed to be the command note of their leader. Then followed a series of cackles from the others, as though they were appraising his judgement.

What a fascinating picture they made! Their wedge-like formation conveyed the idea of tremendous power. Then the wedge began to dissolve into curves and circles. Now it formed a letter S, now a W. At one moment those dark bodies looked like a figure 8. There was no hurry, no confusion; they seemed to melt from one formation into another. Then the curves straightened out again, and that powerful wedge drove its nose once more towards the distant estuary, and I heard their cackles and honkings growing fainter and fainter.

"Silly geese," we say. Yet there is no bird more wary or more cunning. In their trusted leader seems to lie the knowledge of the centuries. Out on the mud-flats of the estuary the wild-fowler pits his skill and his modern weapons against them, and meets with small success, and even when they are feeding inland their human foes are still active.

Pheasant, partridge, grouse shooting some consider sport, but the pursuit of wild geese with some men becomes an obsession. I have watched sportsmen tramping in the cold over tidal marshes with the east wind stinging, to crouch perhaps for hours in some muddy creek. Then there comes at flighting time the sound of whistling wings overhead. For a moment the dark bodies, with necks outstretched, smudge the waning light. The gun flashes, spitting out its venomous hail of bullets. Perchance the thud of a falling goose, the gurgling of the receding tide, the call of a curlew, and the pipe of an oyster-catcher are the only sounds which break the silence.

CHAPTER
TWELVE

The Hirings

It was a lovely morning when Raq and I started out for the farm. Something of the pale sunlight had entered into the heart of all wild things, for there was plenty of life astir, considering that it was Winter time. Blackbirds scratched for their breakfasts where the sodden leaves lay under the trees; wrens popped in and out of the hedges like little brown mice; whilst the chaffinch, with his "pink-pink," seemed the heartiest of them all.

I watched some rooks feeding in a field. One couple interested me particularly, for the old cock indulged in several antics which rather reminded me of his courtship ritual. He became quite gallant, and hopped up to his mate with a sideway step which was almost comic. Perhaps he was reminding her that in a couple of months or so the old urge for nest-making would surge within her, and was telling her that he, on his part, would be quite ready to help.

Raq left the hedge to investigate the fringe of a wood. Everything was so still that I could hear him pattering through the undergrowth. Then a squirrel dashed up the trunk of a fir-tree, and from the first fork looked down and ticked him off for daring to intrude into his sanctuary. When I approached, the little fellow dashed with daring leaps from branch to branch.

Looking over a hedge, with my field-glasses, I saw a brown smudge in the next field. It was a hare. Evidently the damp grass was not to her liking, for she kept stopping to shake the moisture from her hind legs. Then she would sit still and wipe her face with her front paws. All the time, by the quick turning of her ears and the alert movements of her nose, I knew that she was keeping careful watch for enemies.

We pushed on to the farm. As we walked through the fields, it struck me that everything was unusually quiet. I could see no sign of any one either ploughing or hedging, and then I remembered that there had been few signs of human life in the fields we had come through. As I entered the farm Joe appeared. I noticed that he was more "togged up" than is usual in the morning.

"Ye've come at t' reet time," he said with his usual smile. "We can just do with an extra hand on t' farm this week."

"Well," I said, laughing, "you look too togged up for work. The place looks deserted. Are your men on strike?"

"Ye fergit it's 'term' week. There's only me and John and our man at the High Barn left. All t' lads is on

81

holiday. It's hirin' day at Penworth. Coming with us? Ye'll meet a lot o' folks as knows ye. We'll 'ave a bite o' summat, and then get off."

We stopped in the village and picked up Alan. They seemed to get a greeting from everyone we passed, in car or on foot. How much more friendly than town life!

"What happens to the married men who live in cottages on the farms? They don't have to move on every six months, do they?" I asked.

Alan shook his head. "No, they're more or less permanent, and instead of having a week off now at term-time, they get an odd week-end or two any time. They are able in that way to help us to run the farm when all t' lads are on holiday."

"There won't be much farm work done this week then," I said.

"No," said Joe, "we shall just carry on, and look after the stock, which means we've to git up a bit earlier. T' women folk have an easier time, for it means less cookin'."

"Penworth looks pretty lively this morning," I said as we entered the town. The streets were full, but people were not rushing with the speed which is seen in large industrial cities. There was a spirit of liveliness, but it was movement without hurry. Men had time to gather in small groups and exchange courtesies and gossip. Then the groups would disperse as men moved on to attach themselves to another little knot further on. Cars were continually arriving, and then in contrast, I caught sight of an old-fashioned gig with its high seat and patient horse. How knowing he looked! He could have found his way to the hirings without the aid of any rein!

The open space in Sandgate was alive with slowly-moving men, and the lively hum of voices. It fascinated me to watch them. It seemed as though the whole mass was slowly revolving, as men kept winding their way in and out of its small groups.

"Good day, George! How's things? Any of your men stopping on?"

I asked what this last phrase meant, and was told that it applied to the farm hands who were content to stay with the same master for another six months.

"And are all these waiting to be hired?" I asked, pointing to groups of lads and girls about.

Alan nodded. "Those fellers ye see talking first to one lad and then another is farmers trying to hire 'em."

"Asking them what wages they want, I suppose?"

"No," said Joe, "the Wages Board settles that. A lad o' twenty-one is entitled to thirty-seven and six a week, less eighteen shillin's for board and lodgin's. If a lad's under twenty-one his wages is fixed at several shillin's a week less."

"Aye," said Alan, "that's so. So there's a big demand fer these younger fellers, fer many of 'em is as handy as older men. This means that many who have reached twenty-one find themselves left. If ye was to stay till th' end o' t' hirin's ye'd find most unengaged were ower twenty-one."

"Aye," said Joe, "an' ye wouldn't talk long to 'em afore they'd tell ye where they'd send t' Wages Board to if they 'got th' chance'."

I left my friends and mingled with the crowd. Noticing a farmer talking to a lad, I edged nearer.

"Can you plough?" I heard him ask. "Can you milk?" and I think he asked something as to whether he was a good getter-up in the morning. One vital question I did hear distinctly, "Do ye mind doin' a bit o' overtime?"

Alan and Joe came up behind me.

"Learnin' a bit, are ye?" laughed Joe.

"I was learning how it was done," I said; "but tell me, that farmer asked the lad no end of questions, and then just walked off. He looks a likely lad, too."

Alan looked after him, and said, "I reckon he's goin' to ask his last master fer his character. Did I ever tell ye the story aboot them two at t' hirin's? No? Well, when t' farmer had finished askin' questions he went off saying, 'I'll go and get yer character from yer previous master.' When he returned he said to the lad, 'I've got yer character an' thoo'll do alreet.' But the lad replied, 'Aye, but I've been and got thine, an' thoo'll not do.'"

We had a good laugh. It was so typical of what seemed to be going on around us.

Just then the farmer came back and went up to the lad. "Ye'll do alreet," he said, and I saw their hands meet for a moment.

"Is he giving him a tip?" I asked.

"No," said Joe. "He's given 'im a shillin'. That means he's formally engaged him. When once it is accepted, there is no goin' back."

"The King's shilling." I interrupted.

"Summat like it. It's called 'Earls,' that givin' of the shillin' is, but I've no notion what's t' meanin' on't."

"It's an old custom," said Alan. "If you walked round at t' hirings years ago you'd have seen numbers of men chewing straw. When a man was definitely engaged by a farmer he walked aboot wi' a straw in his mouth. It helped other farmers to distinguish those who were already hired. But that old custom isn't seen much now-a-days."

I watched the hired lad talking to others of his own age. They evidently were discussing the new work, for they were looking at his new master. Some of them must have had some experience of him, for they nodded their heads approvingly, and we heard one say, "Aye, an' it's a good meat shop, an' all."

Alan looked at me and winked, and Joe laughed and with a satisfied look on his face rubbed his waistcoat, from all of which I gathered that the lad was going to a farm where the food was good and there was plenty of it.

When we were ready to return to the farm, dusk was beginning to fall, and Penworth was giving itself up to revelry. Fainter and fainter grew the raucous sounds of the roundabouts which were enticing the farm lads and lasses to spend their pence. The receding lights from the fairground winked at us like tiny stars. The music grew fainter and fainter as the road opened up to us like a grey ribbon, inviting us to return to the peace and quiet of the farm.

CHAPTER
THIRTEEN

Snakes

"This is slow work, old man," I said to the dog, as we crept along the side of a hedge, "and hard work, too," I added, as another rush of wind almost forced me back a step.

Raq wagged his tail, saying, "It's better down here than up there, master. I'm nearer the ground than you are. Besides, I have four legs to stand on."

Pausing for breath at a corner of the field where the holly-bushes formed a thick screen, I surveyed the countryside. Nothing could be heard but the roar of the tempest. It swept through the tops of the trees with a sound not unlike the inrush of a mighty sea. The trees, all except the oaks, bowed to the storm. These sturdy growths allowed themselves a little play — the rest swayed and bent before the blast.

"We'll wait here a bit," I said. "If Ned has any letters for Whiterigg, he's bound to come this way."

I crouched at the foot of one of the holly-bushes. Away in the distance I could see the river in flood. Water and wind were playing a great game together. "Let's see if we can sweep that alder out of our path," they seemed to say, and the wave reared its crested head, the wind gave it added power, and together they leaped half-way up its green trunk.

Behind me were the hills — solid, imperturbable, immovable. In vain did the gale hurl itself at their great foreheads. Baffled, it swirled down their ghylls and gullies, and vented its disappointment on the woods at their base. In the distance I heard the crash of some falling monarch. The wind had found a victim.

Along the hedge-side a blackbird ventured from its shelter. The storm seemed to turn it topsy-turvy. For a second I saw only a dishevelled black ball — a mix-up of tail feathers, legs and wings. The next moment it was in the holly-bush above my head. I could see it cowering between the sleek forks of the bush, too frightened even to re-arrange its tangled plumes.

It was at this moment that Ned burst upon us, and as he stood before me I felt that somewhere in his make-up was the solidity of the eternal hills that feared neither zephyr nor gale.

"It's a bit wild," he said, as he sat by me for a breather, "but it's fresh-like." I could have laughed outright at this remark. Ned always accepted unconcernedly, and always found something good to say, about the worst of days.

"I love the sound on't," he said, as it ripped through the hedge. "It allus seems to me as though the wind is tryin' to git back its lost power."

I made no comment. I was loth to disturb his philosophizing.

Raq and I went with the postman on the whole of his round. Conversation was so difficult at times owing to the gale that I should have left him at one point only he said he had something to show me in his garden.

At last his letters were all delivered, and he led me round to the field behind his cottage. Here he paused before a big heap of brushwood which lay on the site of a former stack.

Raq, all alert, thought that we were going to rush a rabbit out of the pile. But a sniff or two round its fringes disillusioned him, and he watched us with wondering eyes, as though pitying us for thinking that anything interesting could be hidden there that his nose could not detect.

Ned carefully removed some thick brushwood. Then with an iron "grip" he raised the straw underneath. Peering in, I could see nothing at first but a few twisted twigs. Then Ned lifted the twigs gently and brought them out into the light.

"Snakes," said I drawing back.

Ned nodded, and grinned, and then tucked them away in the hole.

"Sound asleep until the Spring," he said. "Ever seen anything like that afore?"

I shook my head. "I don't like snakes," I said, as we turned towards the cottage to get out of the wind.

"What ye knows aboot 'em is all wrong likely, I reckon." Ned drew up a chair for me by the fire and Raq stretched himself out on the rug.

"Most folks would 'ave killed them on sight. Poor harmless critturs. Ignerance is the worst enemy o' wild things."

"There are two kinds o' snakes," he continued, settling himself comfortably by the fire, "Venomous —"

"Like the viper," I interpolated, glad to be able to show that I knew a little about the subject.

"An' grass snakes," said he.

"The viper," said I, remembering what I had read, "has a V stamped on the back of its head, and —"

"And a grass snake has a big G printed on't, I reckon?" said Ned, with smiling irony. "I reckon ye'd 'ave to kill the poor brute afore ye could see the letterin'. An' ye can't give it back its life if ye find ye've made a mistake, can ye?"

"That's true," I admitted.

"Ye see," he said, "a grass snake is longer. I've known 'em reach a yard i' length, and they've got a head roond like an egg. A viper's only aboot a foot and a half, and his head isn't nicely curved, but is squarer. He's got dark diamond markin's on his back, and sometimes ye can see a kind o' V — an' all the markin's are joined up together."

He looked at me to see whether I was interested.

"That's a good description," I said.

"Now, a grass snake," he continued, "is gen'rally found near watter — sometimes swimmin' in't, fer he likes fish — and 'e's harmless, only he has a knack o' ex — ex —"

I supplied "exciting" and "existing," but Ned shook his head — these were not the words for which he was searching. "Kind o' sweats," said he, helping me on.

"Exuding," I replied.

Ned nodded happily. "Aye," he continued, "he has a knack o' exoodin' a nasty stink like a toad. It comes from his skin, I reckon, so ye've got to be careful in handlin' him. But apart from that, he'll do ye no damage."

I think he must have seen me looking still rather doubtful, for he said:

"Ye still think that he stings wi' that dartin' tongue o' his, I reckon."

I smiled and Ned continued, "That's only fer explorin'. It's his fingers and nose all in one. Them oot yonder 'll wak' up i' a month or two, and after they've had a feed o' frogs and mice, we'll see 'em aboot somewhere."

I rose to go. Ned smiled and said, "There's one other thing that ye can tell yer missus an' all. When them snakes wants a new suit o' clothes, all they does is to rub their heads agin a stone. It cracks the skin and pushes it back ovver their head — then they simply crawls oot o' their old skin, and finds another ready-made underneath — an' never a misfit neither."

As I passed through the village Sally Stordy's door was shut and there was no lamp lit. I could see the fire burning and the china dogs on the mantelpiece half in shadow and half catching the flickering flame. Thinking that she might be in the yard I opened the door. I called, but received no answer. Just as I was about to go Sally herself came in.

"Ee! I am glad I've caught ye," said she, lifting a bulging string bag and dumping it on the table. Me and Martha, 'er as is married to me 'usband's brother, has bin doin' a bit o' shoppin' in toon. The Sales is on, ye recollect, and we both wanted a few bits o' things. Sit doon and mak' yersel' comfertable. I'll soon have a cup o' tea ready. And what have ye bin up to on a day like this?"

I told her of my round with Ned and the gossip that I had picked up. Lastly I finished by telling her of the snakes asleep under the brushwood.

"Sakes alive!" said she, "but I'm feared o' them things; but I likes to hear aboot 'em all the same."

And so, while Sally busied herself getting the meal ready, she told me a little of her day's outing.

"Talkin' of snakes skinnin' theirsel's," she said laughing, "we went in a grand shop — one o' them places where they calls ye 'madam' — plain 'missus' is good enough fer me. Besides, I reckon ye've got to pay fer all that hanky-panky. But Martha had set 'er heart on a velveteen dress, that were in t' winder, fer 'er holidays. It were all colours o' t' rainbow."

I smiled as I thought of Martha, good hefty Martha, wearing such a frock.

"Well," continued Sally, "we went in, and Martha tried it on. 'First time I've seed myself all at once fer 'ears,' sez she, standin' afore a big lookin'-glass. 'My little 'un at 'ome only shows a bit o' me at a time. What do ye think o' this, Sally-lass?' 'Well,' sez I, not wishin' to hurt 'er feelin's, 'Ye fills it oot pretty well, but ye'd set it off better wi'oot them woollen stockin's and them boots wi' 'lastic sides.'"

Here Sally looked at me, and then laughed as I have seldom heard her.

"Talkin' aboot them snakes, what a job we 'ad gettin' 'er oot o' that dress. It came ovver me as I thowt of 'er bein' skinned. Howsomever, we got her oot on't at last. She were fair disappointed not to 'ave it, but I telled her that such things were not fer the likes o' 'er. 'Them things,' sez I, 'is made fer women who 'as only a front and a back — and no sides to 'em.' Has your missus bin to the Sales?"

Here Sally paused for breath.

"I'm afraid she has, Sally," I sighed. "Going to sleep for the Winter as snakes do has many advantages. It puts folks beyond care, worry — and *temptation*."

Sally smiled, but said nothing. But I am sure she followed my thoughts.

CHAPTER
FOURTEEN

The Red-Throated Diver

A keen white frost had settled on the fields and the air was decidedly "nippy". Raq was searching in vain for something to chase.

"Scent bad, old man?" I asked, as he gazed irresolutely at the hedge. For answer he plunged into the gorse bushes, but only a cock blackbird flew out, scolding him for his intrusion.

What an artist Jack Frost is! How silently his brush works, his filigree seeming to be blown on tree, shrub, and twig. He overlooks nothing. Even the delicate spider-webs do not escape his attention.

As the sun pierced through the mist, I stood and listened to the birds tuning up. It seemed like an orchestra where each player was testing his instrument to see whether it were in tune. The chaffinch was ringing out a couple of notes defiantly as though saying to the thrushes, starlings, and hedge sparrows around, "Take your pitch from me." The yellowhammer protested that he was handicapped by having mislaid the last part of his song.

As the sun gained strength, so the chorus of birds swelled over the fields. Above them all rose the shrill soprano of the misselthrush.

I was startled by the report of a gun. Raq stopped his hunting and stood alert and quivering, his nose searching the air. Then he dashed through the hedge. The next thing I saw was Raq carrying a dead bird to the gamekeeper, John Fell.

"I've too many o' them magpies roond 'ere," he said almost apologetically. "T' missus is feared fer 'er young chickens, an' is allus at me to thin 'em oot a bit."

They're arrant egg stealers, I suppose?"

John nodded. "An' 'cos they can't choose a-tween what they shouldn't touch and what they should, they end this way." Here he lifted up the dapper black and white bird and put it in his bag. "Where was ye makin' for?"

"Anywhere," I answered laconically.

"There's an interestin' bird doon by t' loch, if ye'd care to take a walk."

"What is it?" I asked eagerly.

"A red-throated diver. I reckon it's worth seein' if it's still there. Keep t' dog in to heel and we'll go quietly."

Not a breath stirred the trees as we neared the lake. In the distance I could hear the cackling chorus of wild ducks, and as we neared the reeds I only just prevented

Raq from dashing after a coot. At last we came to an old, dilapidated boathouse, and crept quietly inside. John scanned the waters with my field-glasses.

"Aye," he said at length, "there they are — a couple on 'em. 'Ave a good look, fer they're birds o' passage, an' ye don't often get th' chance."

I focussed my glasses on a couple of duck-like birds about a couple of feet in length — a nice sober study in light grey and white.

"They're not particularly handsome, John."

"No, but ye fergit they're still in Winter dress. When they puts on their weddin' feathers there's a big diffrance. Their 'eads is bluish-grey, and on t' back o' their necks kind o' black mottlins."

"And why are they called red-throated divers? I can't see any red throat."

"That comes on later, an' all — a long band o' chestnut. Look! Summat's frightened 'em."

I was glad I had kept my eyes glued to my field-glasses while talking, for I saw them raise their necks. Their movements fascinated me, for they had the sinuous grace of a serpent. They twisted their necks in every direction, never once making an awkward turn.

"They're sinking under the water, John. Something must have scared them."

"Keep yer eyes on 'em."

Slowly but surely they disappeared under the water. It was not a clean dive, such as the grebe makes. It was more like the quiet settling down of a submarine.

"They look as though they had opened their ballast-tanks and the inrush of water was weighing them down."

John chuckled. "That's it noo. Can ye see their necks and 'eads above t' water? Them's their periscopes. See 'ow all t' other birds 'as made themsel's scarce an' all?"

I swept the lake with my glasses.

"You're right. There's not a duck to be seen."

"Well, look above ye."

For a moment I could see nothing that could have caused the scare. Then I saw the unmistakable flight of a peregrine falcon high above us.

"Owd 'Sudden Death's' aboot. Not even them divers is takin' any liberties wi' him. Watch their necks now."

I had hard work to distinguish the birds, for they were pressing down their heads and necks on the water, and keeping as still as statues.

"All that the peregrine will be able to see is a line on the water, like the ripple of some small wave."

"Aye, 'e's got no target to strike at."

"I suppose they won't breed here, John, will they?"

John shook his head. "I reckon they're on their way now to t' north o' Scotland fer that job."

As we walked home I told John about the wild cat Jerry and I had seen.

96

"Did he tell you about it?" I asked.

"'E did," said the keeper with satisfaction. "An' what's more, th' beggar's danglin' from t' gibbet ower yonder, if ye'd like to see 'im."

"No thank you," I answered hurriedly. "However did you catch it?"

"Well, it were Jerry as found where it were in t' 'abit o' sleepin', in an owd holler tree where 'e could git oot either top or bottom way. There were a kind o' ledge inside, a cosy spot an' all."

"How did Jerry find it?"

"'E 'eard a couple o' jays makin' a divil of a row. So 'e crept up to see what were causin' it. They were flyin' from tree to tree, peerin' and quizzin' into this perticler tree. They'd fly ower the top, and then squawk oot. A farm-lad 'appened to pass, so Jerry sent 'im to fetch me."

"What happened?"

"Well, t' cat must 'ave known 'e were in a fix, fer when Jerry battered on the tree 'e wouldn't stir, so we 'ad to kindle a fire in the bottom 'ole. As soon as smoke got thick 'e come oot at the top an' made a flyin' leap."

"And your gun did the rest, I suppose, poor thing?"

"Aye, it did," said John apologetically.

Leaving John, Raq and I made our way down to the village, though it was getting rather late in the afternoon for visits.

"It's a proper afternoon call ye're makin' an' all," said Sally, as I pushed open her door. "I were wonderin' when I should see ye."

97

"Have you just finished collecting your eggs?" I asked, seeing a number lying on the table.

"I'm just puttin' 'em under a broody 'en. She's aboot ready to sit. I give 'er a pot egg or two yesterda' just to see if she were serious aboot it. She sat tight all reet, so I thowt as 'ow I'd go in an' put these thirteen under 'er when it's dark."

"Does she take to the eggs better if you put them under her at night?"

"Well, it's 'ard to say. Some sez they does and some sez it don't matter, an' that if a 'en means to sit she'd sit on a dozen taters just as well. There were a feller 'ere a year sin' from Birming'am or some sic place, a proper town feller. 'E come to these parts fer 'is 'ealth, pore feller, an' 'e'd a cough worse'n a sheep on turnips, but a reg'lar Mary Ann, I can tell ye. 'E telled me 'e'd an idea to keep a few chickens, so I asked 'im if 'e 'ad a sittin' 'en. 'I'm afraid not, Mrs. Stordy,' sez 'e. Mrs. Stordy, mind ye!" Here Sally gave one of her infectious laughs. "I've never bin called Mrs. Stordy sin' Tom an' I were wed. 'I'm afraid not,' sez 'e, 'all my 'ens keep runnin' aboot.' 'Well, then,' sez I, ''ave ye a cockerel?' 'No, Mrs. Stordy,' sez 'e. 'They mak's too much noise early morning.' So seein' I should 'ave to do a lot o' awkward explainins, I towd 'im I'd see to th' 'ole business fer 'im."

"So you got him a broody hen and all the eggs, did you, Sally?"

Sally nodded. "Aye, pore feller. I set 'im up all reet. An' what do ye think? He got ten pullets oot o' thirteen eggs! 'E died, pore feller; but it were sad to see t' way 'e used to look after them chicks. These 'ere eggs is from 'is pullets. 'E made me 'ave 'em. So I allus thinks of 'im when I'm settin' a broody."

She brushed a tear away with her apron, and then, with her usual smile, started laying the table.

"Here's a bit o' currant nickie I've made," she said.

"That's a new name, Sally. What is it?"

"A plate-cake wi' currants in, instead o' black currants or apples."

I watched her as she lifted down the red tea canister. What a hospitable soul she is. Washing-day, baking-day, market-day, or cleaning-down, never have I found her too busy to lay the cloth.

CHAPTER
FIFTEEN

A Vixen's Earth

As I came up to Jerry's cottage I noticed that he was in his garden. A few crumbs on the ground told me that he had been feeding the birds. I opened the gate quietly, and as I entered, a robin carolled full-throated from the hedge. A moment later he swooped down to the crumbs, stared hard at both Jerry and myself, and seemed to be waiting. Even as he cocked his head on one side his little mate flitted down beside him, and together they shared the food.

"That's the hen," said Jerry, pointing to the second comer. "Ye can only tell which is t' cock when ye sees 'em together."

I compared the two birds for a moment. "She's not quite so ruddy on the breast. That's the only difference so far that I can see," I said.

Jerry nodded. "They'll have a nest shortly somewhere roond aboot," he said with evident satisfaction.

As we left them to finish their breakfast Jerry said, "Did ye know that t' cocks and hens separate fer t' Winter season? T' owd cock goes his way, and she goes hers. Both on 'em sings when they're livin' alone. Now t' Spring's 'ere and they've joined up, that little hen becomes as silent as a mouse. He does all the singin' at present, and he'll see to it that no other robin comes into my garden if 'e can 'elp it."

As we walked up the lane we overtook a young fellow Jerry knew. He told us that he was going to look at some ferrets.

"Old Dick Bell 'as 'em," he said, pointing to a cottage further on. "Come and 'ave a look at 'em, Jerry, and pick a good un fer me."

We went round to the back of the cottage, and Dick Bell came out. As is the custom in the country, conversation turned on everything but the matter in hand. No one would have thought that anything was for sale or that a customer was eager to see the goods. Eventually Jerry walked deliberately towards the large wooden box which stood in a corner of the yard. No sign of life appeared. Then he closed his lips and squealed like a rabbit in pain.

There was a scuffle in the sleeping compartment of the box, and the next moment a lithe brown body rushed out, and a wicked pair of dark eyes blinked at us through the wire-netting.

A moment later four more young ferrets had joined the first one.

101

"They're a nice lot," said Jerry, looking at them critically. "Which one would ye fancy?" he asked, turning to me.

I tried to look at them with the air of "one who knows," and after a moment's critical scrutiny, I pointed to the biggest one of the litter.

"Ye wants a lot fer yer money," said Jerry with a grin, at the same time shaking his head. "Let's have a look at that un, Dick," and he pointed to the one which had rushed out as it heard Jerry's squeal.

Dick opened the door of the hutch, and running his hand up the back, gripped it firmly round the neck with thumb and forefinger. As he did so, the ferret turned his head quickly, but there was no attempt to snap.

"Aye," said Jerry ruminatingly; "nice broad head — that means 'e's got a few 'thinkers' in his brainbox. That big un that ye chose 'ud be clumsier than this un. This 'as a nice medium-sized body and could tackle a rat or a rabbit."

"What aboot that un, Jerry?" asked the young fellow pointing to a ferret still in the hutch; "that un wi' the long pointed snout — 'e looks a smart un?"

Jerry looked at it and shook his head. "'Asn't the brains o' the wide-'eaded un. P'raps 'e'd mak' a quicker worker, but 'e'd not be as sure as this un. If it was me, owd 'wide 'ead' 'ud be my fancy. He were t' fust to answer my squeal — that shows 'e's keen. An' e' warn't vicious when Dick 'andled 'im neither. He'll mak' a useful animal. I'm sartain."

Having delivered his judgement, Jerry gave me a look, and we sauntered off, leaving them to haggle over the price.

As we left the cottage I asked, "What's the best thing to feed ferrets on?"

"A bit o' raw meat and a drink o' milk," said the old poacher promptly.

"Doesn't the red meat make them savage?"

Jerry shook his head decisively. "Meat's t' natural food o' ferrets. Give it 'em, an' they're satisfied. But if ye gives 'em owt else, like bread and milk, then they're allus cravin' fer what they never gits — that's what mak's 'em savage. An' if ye puts a bread-fed ferret down a burrer, and he finds a rabbit there, what happens? He just settles doon to a feed — 'e goes on t' bust while t' farmer clicks his heels together and waits fer an hour or two, mebbe, but a meat-fed un just nips it, and t' rabbit bolts."

"Where are you making for?" I asked Jerry, as we left the lane and turned into a field.

"That wood above Whiterigg, yonder. There's a vixen bin 'angin' roond, and I reckon she's thinkin' o' 'aving some cubs, and John Fell won't be anxious fer 'er to set up house-keepin' so near to his pheasant coverts. Better keep Raq in to 'eel," he added; "there may be a trap o' two in them hedges. I know John's after t' rats, and there may be a bit o' poison lyin' aboot an' all."

Passing through a gate Jerry held up his finger. From the hedge there poured forth a merry roundelay.

"Toll-loll-loll-loll-loll — glad-to-see-you-here," piped the singer.

"Chaffinch," I said.

"Good," said he; "I reckon that's the first time ye've heard his song since afore Christmas. Turn yer money ower in yer pocket just fer luck like."

The little soloist came into view, and we stopped to admire his jauntily raised blue crest and the fire which glowed on his rounded breast. His hop from branch to branch had the suggestion of a strut, and we could see the gleaming white slash on his wings.

"He's a diff'rent lookin' feller to what he was a couple o' months back," said Jerry admiringly. "Ye could 'ardly pick 'im oot from t' sparrers then. He's gotten 'is Spring suit on now."

I put Raq on the leash when we entered the wood. The deadness of Winter had vanished, and though the bracken still drooped and the trees showed little sign of real life, yet the honeysuckle bore tender leaves. Peeping out from the dead undergrowth shy green shoots were showing the tips of their fingers.

Finally we stood before a hole which looked like an enlarged rabbit-hole.

"This is where she's thinkin' a' 'avin' her fam'ly," said Jerry. "Would ye 'ave thowt it were a fox-hole?"

"Well," I answered, "it's certainly bigger than that usually made by a rabbit."

"Aye, it is," Jerry said; "an' ye niver saw a rabbit leave a pile o' earth right i' front o' its door neither. He gen'rally wants to enter mighty quick, and a 'eap o' sand blockin' the way might mean death to 'im."

"And doesn't a fox find it inconvenient as well?"

"It 'as its compensations," answered Jerry. "Ye see, if a terrier wants to gets in, that 'eap o' earth mak's him go in a bit askew like — an' if t' fox is waitin' fer 'im inside, there's more likelihood o' t' fox seizin' 'old o' 'is muzzle if 'e comes in a bit on t' slant."

I bent down to the hole.

"Do you think she's inside now?"

The poacher knelt down and sniffed up the burrow. "Can't smell owt. Let Raq 'ave a try."

But Raq did not seem to be particularly interested.

"I could tell ye soon enough if I 'ad yon ferret o' Dick Bell's. If t' vixen were at 'ome and we put owd 'wide 'ead' at t' entrance, he'd stick his fur oot like a 'edgehog — but 'e wouldn't go in no matter what ye did. I'll 'ave to tell John Fell."

"And what will he do?" I asked.

"Oh, he'll stink her oot o' this un, and then mebbe 'e'll find 'er another."

"But suppose she won't use it. You can't make a vixen settle down just where you like, can you?"

Jerry did not answer for a moment.

"No," he said, "I don't say as ye can. But if she's bin shifted from two or three earths, an' 'er cubs are a'most ready to be born, an' there's one earth as is fresh an' clean, an' all t'others stink like h— — (beggin' yer pardon) — then she's getting pretty desp'rate, to my way o' thinkin', and she'll tak' the one that John mak's fer 'er."

We did not talk much as we walked homewards. The thought of that vixen seeking about desperately for a refuge rather haunted me. I know Jerry, too, must have been thinking similarly, for as we parted he said, "She'll be all right noo. I'll see that she gits a better place than yon hole in t' wood — sort o' place that any mother ought to 'ave. So never worry yersen aboot her."

CHAPTER
SIXTEEN

The Steel Trap

Raq scampered ahead joyously as I turned towards Sally Stordy's cottage, and I saw him push her door open with his nose.

When I arrived a moment later I heard her laughing, and found Raq standing over a small puppy which lay on its back on the mat in front of the fire.

"What's this?" I asked. "An addition to the household?"

Sally nodded. "Aye, oor Jimmy brought it 'ome a week or two sin'. Bill Flather give it 'im — its mother is yon black and white dog 'e runs wi' 'is sheep. 'E were goin' to drown t' pups, but oor Jimmy begged for one, and so 'ere it is."

I picked up the puppy and looked at it critically.

"What do ye mak' on't?" Sally asked.

"Well," I said slowly, "it isn't what I might truthfully describe as a thoroughbred, Sally. I was just trying to make out what he was."

She laughed, and I knew by her tone that she had already taken it into her big heart.

The puppy seemed to know we were discussing the big question of pedigree, and looked up at us with the misty blue eyes of young puppyhood, one ear slightly cocked.

"By his muzzle and chest I should say that there was a bit of bull terrier in him. But the sheep-dog shows in his ears. His hair is like an Irish terrier's, and his legs are like either a Sealyham's or an Aberdeen's. I should say, Sally, that he was a pure-bred *Multum-in-parvo*."

"What's that?" she asked. "I've never 'eerd tell on't afore."

"It means," I said smiling, "much in little."

It was good to hear her laugh. She threw back her head, and if ever a body radiated kindly mirth she did.

She picked up the puppy, hugged it, and, holding it at arm's length, said, "Ye may not be a beauty, and ye'll niver win a prize, but ye've more sense than some on 'em, and Sally'll look after ye, love."

"You needn't worry about his sense. Speaking generally, a good cur has more real brains than many a thoroughbred, and if they've got sense and affection, what does it matter what they look like?"

"I only 'ope 'e 'as eyes like your Raq — soft brown 'uns as talks to ye wi' every blink of 'em." At the mention of his name Raq stopped playing to give Sally a lick. "Them two 'as takken to each other already," she said.

And so while she warmed me with a cup of hot tea, the dogs played together. "Multum" grew more and more bold, until at last, when I rose to go, he was hanging on to Raq's ears and being lugged round the kitchen.

★ ★ ★

We made our way to where I thought I should find the gamekeeper, John Fell. He was not far from his usual haunts, looking over the top of a wall very intently.

He nodded a welcome, and then pointed to the far end of the field. "There's summat oot-o'-th'-ordinary goin' on doon yonder. See them small birds flittin' aboot excited like ower yon bush?"

"Yes. What do you think all the pother is about?"

We were quite two hundred and fifty yards away, yet we could distinctly hear the excited chatter of the birds.

"What can ye mak' oot wi' yer glasses?"

"There's something in the bottom of the bush the birds seem to be angry with. You have a look," I said, handing him the binoculars.

"Aye, it's either a weasel or a stoat, I reckon, an' they're mobbin' 'im."

"They can't do him much harm anyway."

"That's true," he said, handing back the binoculars, "but they can mak' 'im feel uncomfortable. Ye see, they're drawin' the attention o' the whole countryside to 'im, an' 'e don't like it. By Jingo!" — he seized the glasses again hurriedly — "it's no weasel; it's an otter. Come on," he said, quickly climbing the wall, "an' keep that dog well into heel — if ye don't want a slice takken oot on 'im."

We all rushed down the field pell-mell, and as we neared the bush, I saw that John was right. An otter came into view, moving so slowly that we soon overtook him. The cause of his slowness was only too evident. The poor beast was dragging along a rabbit trap which was gripping his front paw.

We circled round him as best we could. Whenever Raq moved the otter stood at bay, and I caught sight of the fangs which would soon have "takken a slice oot on 'im."

"Whatever can we do to release him, John?"

"I 'ardly knows what to do fer the best."

But the next moment he had stripped off his coat. "Walk in front of 'im wi' Raq an' attract 'is attention," he directed, and whilst the otter veered round to face Raq, John stepped up behind him and with a dexterous

throw covered him with his coat and held him. I saw his right hand move swiftly up the otter's back towards the neck, as he did in seizing a ferret. Holding him by the scruff of the neck, he pinioned the otter's head to the ground.

"Fling back the coat," he shouted. "Quick!"

Holding Raq with one hand it wasn't an easy job, but I jumped in and did as I was told. John then put his foot down on the spring, releasing the terrible steel teeth, and threw the poor beast lightly towards the hedge.

Without once looking round, the otter picked himself up, and with an odd shuffling, waddling motion, disappeared through the hedge into the maze of tangled undergrowth.

"You did that well, John," I said, admiringly. "Did you notice if he was very badly hurt?"

"I don't think he'd been in long, fer as far as I could see 'is foot warn't much swollen. Just a bit of broken flesh, and not much blood aboot."

I felt by then that it was safe to loosen Raq. He immediately got on the trail of the vanished otter, but I called him back. On the whole, he did not show a very lively interest in the scent of the trail.

"The poor thing was a long way from the river, John. What do you think he's been doing up here?"

"Ye can tak' my word fer it, an otter mak's very long journeys by night when it wants to. 'Untin' fer food in t' river is pretty difficult fer 'im this 'ard weather."

"But the river has not been completely frozen over this year, John."

"That mebbe. But when t' frost is severe there ain't much fish fer 'em in t' watter. I've told ye afore 'ow an otter is fond of eels, but eels buries theirsels in t' mud this weather, and the trout goes inter their 'idin'-places an' all."

"But there'll be salmon up from the sea, and that's good enough fare for anybody."

"Aye, they've come up from the sea reet enough, but they don't get to these 'igher reaches o' t' river until April or May. So I reckon yon pore feller left t' riverside to see what 'e could pick up along t' hedge-bottoms. 'E's nowt but a water-weasel, an' first cousin to the stoat an' all. An' that'll tell ye what 'e can do in the way o' eatin'. Nowt comes amiss to 'im — rats, rabbits, voles, or water'ens, frogs or chickens. I've knowed an otter travel as many as twelve miles at night on a foragin' expedition."

John paused for a moment. "I shouldn't wonder if —"

"What, John?" I asked.

"I just bethought me that yon would be a dog-otter foragin' fer 'er and t' young 'uns. They'll be in a sad case when 'e returns empty-'anded, an' wi' a wounded foot."

"But is this the time of year that they have young ones?"

"There's no real time. I've found 'em all through t' year, but ginrally speakin' just aboot early Spring there'll be youngsters aboot. An' the queer thing is that t' young 'uns don't like eatin' fish at first. They prefers flesh, an' they've a'most got to be weaned to fish food."

"Then it looks as though the old weasel instinct in them is uppermost if the youngsters take naturally to flesh. Perhaps that is why this otter was ranging so far afield. Perhaps he could have caught fish easily, but was hunting abroad to get the little beggars what they preferred. They may have been turning up their noses at fish."

John laughed hilariously — a most unusual thing for him to do.

"I allus feels glad," he said almost apologetically, "when I can do a good turn to a wild crittur."

"You are both a game preserver and a game keeper, John," I said enthusiastically.

He answered nothing, but I knew he was pleased.

112

CHAPTER
SEVENTEEN

Early Lambs

There was still a good deal of snow lying about as I set out for the farm. It was hard walking, and I slipped more than once. Where the dog had walked I could see the deep marks of his claws, and admired Nature's resourcefulness, giving him such non-skid feet. On some roads the snow-plough had been at work, and I was thankful for the relief it gave in walking. I left the road at one point and cut up by the side of a hedge, but after extricating Raq from a snow-drift, I decided to keep to the well-defined paths.

After passing a cottage by the roadside, a carrion crow flew up from the bottom of the hedge. He carried a white egg in his strong beak. He was so close to me that I could actually see how he carried it. It was not between the upper and lower bill, as I expected, but the cunning old rascal had thrust his lower bill through the egg-shell, and then closed the upper one on it.

I slipped through the gate, and searching in the bottom of the hedge found a hen's nest with seven eggs still left in it. So I walked back to the cottage to inform the owner.

"There's a 'doup' just visited the nest up there, and carried away a hen's egg," I said to the woman whom I knew by sight.

"Was it by yon gate?" she asked.

"Yes, and those left will not be there long if you leave them."

"It'll be yon Ancona that's bin layin' away. I've noticed 'er slinkin' off a time o' two. But she's that cunnin' I've not bin able to find 'er nest. Thank ye fer tellin' me."

"I shouldn't leave them very long," I said, "or he'll get the lot. You'll find which nest it is quite easily as I've trampled the snow down round it."

At last, tired with the heavy walk, I caught sight of the farm chimneys, with their blue smoke curling straight upwards.

In the fields the black Galloway cattle had trodden down the snow. A shed stood waiting to give them shelter, but it seemed as though they scorned such comforts and preferred to trust to their shaggy coats, rather than to the roofs of man's devising.

Joe was just entering the yard, and he gave a whoop of delight as he caught sight of me.

"Well, who'd have thowt of seein' you oot on sic a day," he exclaimed.

"I thought you might all need digging out, so I came along to do my good deed," I said laughingly.

"Come in and have a warm. Sally's got summat as'll set you goin' again." And so round the table we sat enjoying the good things brought out of the larder.

"I suppose the lambing season has begun, hasn't it?" I inquired anxiously.

"Aye, we're just nicely started. About a dozen have arrived," said Joe.

"And how many have you — ewes, I mean?"

"Two hundred, so there'll be a bit o' work afore they've all settled doon with their fam'lies."

"I was trying to tell a friend of mine what breeds of sheep you stock, but there seemed to be so many. I got as far as a Border Leicester Tup, but I couldn't for the life of me remember what breed the ewes were. I nearly said Shorthorns in despair."

Joe laughed. "Even *you* couldn't cross an owd sheep wi' a milkin' coo. What ye were trying to think on were mebbe Grey-faced Leicester Cross. We used to cross a Grey-faced Wensleydale wi' —"

"Here, that's enough for the present, Joe."

After a warm up, Joe and I went out to see the sheep, leaving Raq before the fire. Passing through the gate which leads from the farmyard, I recalled the view one gets in Summer. The land falls away towards the river, not in sweeping flatness, but in rich heaving undulations, as though loth to lose its height. Almost every summit is crowned with larch, pine, and elm. In the valley below, the river glides reflecting the moods of hills and fields. Then once again the land begins to rise, until at last the distant hills seem to hold up the very sky itself.

But no such view spread out before Joe and me. Only a white desert, relieved by trees, which stood out fantastically black and white.

"Do you bring in your ewes to some farm-building when you are expecting the lambs to arrive?"

Joe shook his head. "We find they're better left to theirsel's. Some farmers with a small stock sometimes bring 'em up to a Dutch barn, but we leave 'em oot."

I watched two tiny straggly-limbed youngsters sheltering behind their mother.

"They look as though a puff of wind would blow them over."

"Aye, ye'd think so to look at 'em. But as a matter of fact, once they get on their legs, and get a drop o' warm milk into 'em, it can rain, hail or snow, and they're all reet. If a new lamb's gettin' plenty o' milk, it can stand more cold than its mother can."

Once again I stood and looked at them. Is there anything more appealing than to see those long tails waggling like catkins as the warm milk streams down their thirsty throats?

"The milk must be very rich to give them strength to resist the cold. Is it stronger than cow's milk, Joe?"

"I reckon it is, and if ye watch 'em ye'll find their motto is 'little and often'. The lie o' this land is a help an' all. D'ye see how it rises and slopes? It means that whichever way t' wind blows, the ewes can get a sheltered spot. We allus cart the turnips to where it's warmest, fer sheep are silly things."

"In what way do you mean, Joe?"

116

"They allus seem when left to theirsel's to get to the most exposed part o' t' field. I reckon it's because they never face a storm; they allus turns their tails to it, and so they get driven before it. So one of my jobs, every night, last thing, is to drive them to a warmer corner."

The bleats of the lambs broke the silence, punctuated by the lower raucous bleating of the ewes.

"I should be tempted if I were a farmer to bring the sheep all up and put them under cover, especially if I had such good outbuildings as you have, Joe."

Joe laughed. "There speaks the townsman, used to coddlin' hissel'. I don't mean you," he added hastily, linking his arm in mine. "But if I were to put a lot of ewes and their lambs together in a small space, we should soon be in bigger difficulties than facin' bad weather. Just picture what 'ud happen. Here's a ewe with two lambs, and she's near one as hasn't any. What happens? The one as hasn't any pinches one o' 'ers. Then, mebbe, a few hours later her own couple arrives, an' she finds hersel' wi' three to look after."

"Well, can't you give the pinched one back again to the rightful mother?"

"Aye, it sounds easy enough, but the trouble is that the mother won't 'ave it back once it's bin separated from her for a few hours. So there ye are."

★　★　★

We returned to the farm, to receive a great welcome from Raq. Then we went into the dining-room, where a huge log threw out its grateful warmth. Of course we had to eat again, and then have the usual "crack," but things did not seem quite complete somehow. Nothing was said. Then to our delight we heard Alan's footsteps and cheery voice in the kitchen, and the party round the fire was complete as of old.

Later we found ourselves listening to the wireless. When at home I listen to the weather report very casually, but how intently Alan and Joe listened! When we heard the announcer foretell warmer conditions and more normal temperature, Alan said — "Hundreds o' farmers and shepherds 'll say 'Thank God' when they hear that," and I then realized for the first time what a boon such forecasts were in the country.

As I went up to bed I looked up at the distant fells. Had the shepherds before the big fall of snow received the warning of the wireless, and with their faithful dogs brought their flocks down to the lowlands in time?

"Star gazing?" said Joe as he passed me on the landing. I told him my fears.

"I reckon there'll be a few sheep buried up there," he said.

"That means a loss to the farmer," I sympathized.

"Not always. So long as a thaw doesn't set in, sheep can live together under t' snow fer several days. Ye see, t' snow's light and doesn't shut oot the air, an' they come oot not much t' worse fer bein' under it. But thawing snow thickens an' smothers 'em."

118

"But how can they find the sheep in such a wilderness?"

"Ye fergit their dogs, brave lil' fellers. They'll scent 'em oot all right — an' then it's just diggin' work. O' course, there's allus other dangers when t' sheep is buried. Foxes are ravenous with hunger, and if they find them they soon get a meal, eatin' their legs first. Or if by any chance t' sheep begin strugglin' under t' snow, and then manage to poke their heads out — then mebbe there's a carrion crow waitin' to pick their eyes oot."

The candle I had carried up with me warned me that it was time to say "Good-night." So I made my way to my room, where my feather-bed waited to envelop me. Candle light! How beautiful it is. Electric light has its advantages, but it invites one to keep awake, whereas a candle is the essence of drowsiness. Electric light scorns shadows, and shadows speak of dreamland, mystery, and twilight, and are a rest to tired eyes.

Before getting into bed I looked through my window. There was a dark streak amidst the white of the snow. It was Daleraven Beck singing its song of eternal freedom.

CHAPTER
EIGHTEEN

The Rising of Trout

April — what power a name has to change our outlook! Yesterday it was wet, and we remarked that it was "raining as usual". But to-day the new month has arrived, and what we once called "rain," now we re-christen with the more hopeful name of "showers".

April — month of opening, month of bird-music, hedges starred with primroses, and woods swaying with bluebells, and the tiny cups of anemones shivering delightedly in the caress of the south-west wind.

I walked up to John Rubb's shop and found him in his office with a large ledger open before him. He welcomed me with his usual genial smile, closed the book with a hopeful bang, and within a few moments we had decided to go down to the river.

"Overhauled all your trout tackle?" he asked, as I left him to make certain preparations for the outing. I assured him that all my paraphernalia was in good order. "If you have faulty stuff ye're almost sure to hook the biggest fish o' your life on it and so lose it," he said as I left him.

★   ★   ★

An hour later we were in the Morris, with Raq seated behind, but not looking so comfortable as he used to do in the old Ford. I don't think he liked the smell of the new leather.

"It doesn't feel quite the same as in the old 'bus," I said to John. "This new car makes me feel a bit shabby too. I wish it weren't quite so smart."

"It's had its first knock though," said John, pointing to the right mudguard. There was no regret in his tone. I rather thought there was a tinge of relief about it, and though he said no more, it rather reconciled me to the new order of things. The new car was not going to be a pampered luxury. The first dent had destroyed its newness, and henceforth its spick-and-span appearance would no longer tyrannize. It was to be a servant, not a master, and take us everywhere as the old Ford did.

Before running the car into a quiet lane, we paused on a bridge. We sat for a moment or two listening to the tinkle of the waters, their muffled bells, the whisperings of its nymphs and dryads. As we waited, a big heron, with lazily moving wings, passed overhead, and seeing no sign of danger, planed down to a deep pool which lay about a hundred yards from the bridge.

"Watch her," said John, "she'll show you how to fish."

The bird alighted about ten yards from the edge of the pool. For a few moments it stood perfectly still. It was difficult to imagine that it was a living creature. It looked like a grey rock with a cleft or two of shadow in it.

"She's moving," said John, giving me a nudge.

I kept my eyes glued on the grey-blue form. John was right. The bird was gliding with stealthy footsteps towards the water — moving so quietly and smoothly that it was difficult to detect its progress.

When it was about five yards from the pool it again stood like a statue, and then continued its stealthy approach to the water.

"That's a lesson for both of us," said John, as we moved on. "She's an angler too — one o' the cunningest — and ye saw how quietly she took up her position. There was no footfall that the fish could hear — hardly any movement that they could see. She roused no suspicions. That's the way to go down to your stream, my boy," he added, giving me a knowing and appreciative wink.

After we had "tackled up," and as we parted to fish different parts of the river, John said, "Remember the trout are not too strong yet. Don't spend too much time on the strong streams. Ye'll find 'em in the slower movin' water — and keep out o' sight."

Raq and I set off for a favourite stream of mine. The trees were still bare, but the hazel catkins were swinging their pendulous "lambs' tails," and the honeysuckle was putting forth its tender green leaves. The fields were alive with moving energy. Aloft, the larks were singing out their morning challenge. A kingfisher flashed by me, and I watched it alight on a small branch — the bird eyed me narrowly. What marvellous plumage — what shimmer and sheen!

Here and there strength was being tested. Some wanderer from the South was fancying a field already in possession and the sounds of passionate protest and angry bickering interspersed periods of song.

Here and there I could see a couple of gulls flying over the fields. From side to side they kept turning their heads, hoping to find the dainty morsel of a plover's egg.

Finally I reached the shining pool. Raq took up his usual position on the bank, and must have wondered at the unusual care with which I, thinking of the heron's strategy, approached the water.

No one but an angler knows the real joys of the river. The ear is lulled by a thousand cadences and

whisperings; from the water there rises a soft mossy aroma; the eye looks upon fairy grottoes not seen from the bank, and if one stands still, birds and beasts approach very near, curious to know what the truncated form really is.

Even as my cast carried its tempting lures to the lazy streams under the bushes, I noted the wren exploring the shadowed rootlets. Above me a robin poured forth

123

its Spring litany — not the thin mandoline solo of December, but something richer, fuller, as though it were telling the world that what it prophesied in Winter had all come true.

So I fished the waters, but with little success. Then a tug came to my line, and I felt that I had struck a good fish. Out of the corner of my eye I could see the dog prancing with excitement on the bank. He knew when sport began as well as I did.

But the keen struggle that I expected from the "bite" never matured, and in a moment I was "reeling in" a big chub, instead of the trout for which I had hoped.

"Skelly," I said disgustedly, as I opened the big sucking mouth and carefully extracted the hook.

Whilst adjusting my tackle, I placed the fish on the grass. Raq came near and put his nose down to what he thought had an unusual smell. The chub immediately flopped up, and his tail struck the dog on the nose. It was ludicrous to see the look of surprise on Raq's face, and then to see him rub himself in the grass in order to sweeten that sensitive organ from slime and fishiness.

At first I thought of giving the chub his liberty. I knew he would take no harm from being caught, and suffer little inconvenience from being hooked, because on one occasion, after a big trout had rushed away with my tackle in his jaws, he had been recaught by a brother angler a couple of hours later, who handed over to me my lost possession. Therefore on the spur of the moment I placed the chub in a pool which the river had

124

left, intending to show him to John when we had our lunch together.

I fished on without much luck. Then towards mid-day, a tiny dimple showed itself on the stiller water. This was a good sign. A trout had risen from the depths at something which had floated overhead.

A moment later I knew what was luring them to the surface, and I saw a beautiful fly coming downstream. Its wings were like a spic-and-span yacht, pale smoky blue in colour. Over the rough water it sailed, buoyant as a cork. Brave little voyager, to trust itself to a stream so turbulent! Into the hollows and on the crests the "Blue Dun" appeared, to be hurried into the quieter water under the bushes. A swirl appeared just behind it — a trout had risen at it and missed his aim by a fraction of an inch. But the little chap was not to escape, for the next moment as its speed slackened the water opened beneath it — and it was not.

Soon the river around me was alive with rising fish. The table was spread for the feast, for the flies had come down in scores, and in no uncertain manner did they rise to it.

One by one speckled beauties found their way into my creel. Then as though a bell had rung and given the alarm, the fish refused to rise. The fly was off the water. The gorged trout retired to the holes and gullies. Their hour of rest had come.

After John and I had had lunch together, I showed him the chub which still rested in the pool.

"I've seen chaps who do 'coarse fishing' catch 'em wi' queer stuff," said he, with all the scorn which a fly fisherman shows for such tactics. "Aye," he continued, "boiled potatoes and cheese, and even shrimps they'll use."

"Better give him his liberty," I said, taking the fish out and placing him in the shallows of the river.

For a moment he lay there resting on his side, and we had time to admire his golden-bronze beauty. Then he righted himself, and with one quick stroke of his powerful propeller was lost in the depths.

John stood looking in the water, and I could see that he was busy thinking. "I've often wondered," he said at last, "why fish which have so many enemies are polished so bright. You've caught roach and perch, haven't you?" he asked.

I nodded, one a shiny beauty with a dark back, and the other olive green with four or five perpendicular striped shadows on its sides.

"Did you notice," asked my friend, "how dull that chub looked when in that pool, and how bright it looked when lying on its side in the river?"

I confessed that I had not.

"Ye see," said John, "they're evidently built on the mirror principle. When that chub was in that pool with a mud bottom, them shining scales reflected mud. When it's on gravel, they'll be tinged with yellow, blue, or pink, according to the stones beneath it. That means that they're well-nigh invisible when they're on an even keel."

126

"And the perch has its stripes," I added, "because it moves about amongst the weeds."

John nodded. "Same as the tiger has living in the jungle. The fish look pretty obvious to us when we've got 'em on dry land. But think what a softenin' effect the water must have — it'll act like a cloud, blurrin' 'em from all their enemies."

After leaving John in town I could not resist stopping before a fish-shop on my way home. I could see what John had called the "mirror principle" written large on every fish. Here were the cod, with white undersides, whilst their backs were greyish brown. The mackerel, with dark green backs of a silken sheen, and their sides and keel of aluminium. The plaice and soles, however, were all "roof and ceiling." They were accustomed to lying flat on the sand, and so their top side was muddy brown. Nature did not waste any paint on their underside — that was milky white and seldom seen. A scarlet lobster stood out from amongst the rest, like a pillar-box. But then his natural colour is indigo, something like the shadowed blueness of the depths in which he lurks.

CHAPTER
NINETEEN

The Fox Evicted

Away in the distance I espied a well-known figure walking very slowly up and down the hedgeside. My binoculars showed me that it was the keeper, John Fell. He had a long stick in his hand and kept peering into the bottom of the hedge.

As Raq and I got nearer I gave him a call, and he beckoned. So I put the dog on the leash. Alas, for him the days of his random wanderings are limited as soon as April comes in.

"What have you lost, John?" I asked.

For answer he took me along the hedgeside to where, opposite a small white withy and concealed in the grass so that no passer-by might notice, lay the olive eggs of a pheasant.

"That's what I'm lookin' fer," he said, "an' a tirin' business it is an' all, keepin' yer eyes glued to t' hedge-bottom, an' they're not ower plentiful as yet."

"Why don't you take the eggs now? I suppose you want them to put under sitting farmyard hens, or in an incubator, don't you?"

"That's the idee. I shall come this way back. If I was to pick 'em up now, ye see, I should have to carry 'em twice the distance."

We wandered up and down the hedgeside for some time. Then John led the way to the fox's "earth" Jerry and I had already investigated.

"By the litter that's lying around I should think there's a fairly big family inside," I said.

John nodded. "Aye, I reckon there is, but they're on the smallish side yet. I shall have to think o' shiftin' 'er and 'er family afore long."

"Too near your pheasant-rearing field, is she?"

"Aye, when ye're bringin' oot a few 'underd pheasants, ye don't want a 'ungry vixen wi' a large family to feed 'anging aboot. I'll 'ave to shift 'er. I've started by givin' 'er notice already."

"What do you mean, John?"

"First of all, I 'ad to find another 'ouse fer 'er. It's not fair sellin' 'er up 'ere, so to speak, wi'oot providin' another fer 'er, so I've got one farther away where's she's not likely to be so troublesome."

"Are we far from it? I should like to see it. What does Big Ben say?"

The keeper pulled out his watch, and smiled. He always remembered what I christened his watch the first time I saw it — one of those big, clumsy old-fashioned turnip-shaped silver watches one never sees in town.

"It'll not tak' us so long. Ye can let Raq off that lead a bit, so long as ye keep 'im from rangin' aboot too far."

As we walked across the sunlit paths, we laughed time and again at the plovers as they dived at Raq when he pryed too closely into their private affairs. How he scuttled off with his tail between his legs!

"It's a good thing that plovers' eggs are protected by law now, John. I've never thought they were any better than a nice fresh hen's egg."

"That's 'cos ye 'adn't paid a guinea fer an early clutch on 'em," he answered, chuckling. "Them fellers in London as used to buy 'em 'ad to keep tellin' theirsels as they ate 'em 'ow much each spoonful cost 'em. They were eatin' what other folks couldn't afford to buy, an' that give 'em a better flavour an' all. What's yon dog after now?"

We saw Raq standing with his nose down to something on the ground, whilst the shrieks of an enraged bird overhead told us that he must have found a nest.

I called him "to heel," and we found that a couple of plover's eggs was the cause of all the disturbance.

"'Ave ye ever found a tern's nest on the shingle by the sea-shore?" John asked.

"Yes, scores of them. I photographed some terns' nests a few years ago. The eggs are something like the plovers', only a little lighter in colour."

"Aye, and not so pointed. I reckon 'underds o' terns' eggs 'as bin sold fer plovers', an' a few gulls' eggs an' all. Folks that pays fer 'em ain't none the wiser. Ye allus tastes jist what ye thinks ye're eatin'."

Soon we arrived at the hole John had prepared, hoping the vixen would bring her young family.

"I see you've scraped out the soil pretty well. You'll be moving this mound from the entrance, I suppose?"

John shook his head. "A vixen allus leaves a mound like yon in front o' t' entrance. Mebbe it mak's any enemy approach it at an angle, an' if she's waitin' inside to snap 'is napper off, it tak's 'im at a disadvantage."

"Oh yes! so Jerry told me. I was asking Jerry how you'd evict her."

"Just before dusk I shall keep droppin' nice young rabbits between 'ere an' 'er old 'ole. She'll soon wind 'em, and foller 'em, an' think 'erself lucky."

"Getting food for the cubs without hunting for it, you mean?"

"Aye, an' she'll mak' up 'er mind when she's on the hunt allus to go t' same way, an' then I'll put t' young rabbits somewhere near this new 'ole."

I looked round the land in which we stood. Even at that moment Raq was busy trying to dig out a rabbit that had dashed to earth, and I saw scores of rabbit-holes wherever I looked.

John smiled. "I'm 'ticin' 'er to where there's plenty on 'em, ye're thinkin'. Well, there's mebbe summat i' that, but once she's removed 'ere, she'll range further afield than these burrers for food."

"But you haven't told me how you will finally get her to quit, John?"

"I'll wait fer some nice evenin' when there's a promise o' darkness, but not blackness, an' when I'm as sure as I can be that there'll be no rain. Then I'll walk quietly to where they're lyin' up, an' sprinkle a drop or two o' lavender water around t' entrance."

"You mean Renardine — the elixir of stink," I said laughing.

"That'll mak' t' owd vixen oneasy-like. As she smells the tainted earth she'll mebbe think she must shift, and she'll see in 'er mind this new 'ome 'to let,' ready wi' provisions. Ten chances to one she'll grab one o' them youngsters by t' scruff o' t' neck and carry 'im off an' plank 'im doon in t' new 'ole, and then go back fer t' others."

"You talk as though you enjoy the whole business, John," I remarked, for he had displayed unusual animation for him. As a rule he is rather matter-of-fact.

He laughed. "I reckon I likes pittin' me wits against a fox's. I likes to see 'em reasonin' it all oot, and all the time they're doin' what ye're wantin' 'em to do."

"Be sure and let me know what happens, won't you?" I said as I left him.

John went back to find more pheasants' nests, and Raq and I walked on, just pottering about with that delightful consciousness that we had nowhere to make for, and could take our time getting there.

On all sides there were signs that birds were in the grip of Spring madness. Skylarks soared aloft and sprayed the ground with glittering drops of music. A moment later one of them was driving an intruder from the small estate to which he laid claim. Every change in the wind will bring to us new bird-visitors and consequent quarrels, for our resident larks have now staked out their territories and will fight for them against those who have migrated from afar.

In almost every field we entered, a pair of partridges would flutter away into their neighbours' land. They were always in pairs. Then bickering would ensue again, and I could hear the rightful claimants protesting against the invasion of their rights, and I seemed to hear the others asking what else they could be expected to do when a huge man and a fierce dog came into their field unawares.

Perhaps what gave me the Spring feeling more than anything else was to see the wood-pigeon, with his burnished neck sparkling in the sun, suddenly soar aloft on smiting wings, and then plane down again in fancy curves. Such is their way of saying that it is good to be alive, and also of course, of telling some lady-love who perches on the pines that there never was a bird who could make so brave a show as himself.

And so we sauntered on until daylight began to wane and the cock-pheasant sounded his raucous curfew — sauntered on with the feeling and wonder that though I had seen many Springs, yet never had I seen one more beautiful.

CHAPTER
TWENTY

New Nests

From the lane in which Raq and I were walking I caught sight of a large nest of sticks securely built in the top of a tree. I saw a couple of magpies flying away, and thinking there might be eggs I climbed up to it.

I found that it was easier to climb the tree than to get my hand into the nest. Thorns protected it at every point. The bird could not have made it more formidable had it been built with barbed wire.

Whilst I was sucking my scratches, I saw Raq suddenly throw his nose up into the air and turn towards the thicker part of the wood. I knew by the way his tail wagged quickly that he had caught the scent of a friend. Then I heard the faint snapping of a twig, and a moment later I caught sight of Jerry threading his way through the undergrowth.

"Owt in?" he asked, looking up.

"Yes," I answered, "but how many eggs there are I can't say. I can only just touch them with my finger-tips."

"Yon's not a nest; it's a fortress, I reckon. Did ye notice what it were built wi'?"

"Sticks and earth —"

134

"That's the cement to 'old 'em together," he interpolated.

"And I rather fancy that the eggs were lying on some wool or hair."

He examined my hands. "Ye'd better come wi' me and get a bit o' salve on them 'ands. They are in a mess," he added.

So we walked back to his cottage, and Jerry rubbed in some salve he said he had made from "leaf lard an' docken leaves," and that it "were good fer owt — rheumatiz, chilblains, stings — owt that needed rubbin' or 'ealin'."

As we came out of the cottage a hoarse guttural rattle came from the wood.

"I reckon them 'magpies' are larfin' at ye," said he. "If that ain't mock'ry, then I'm a Dutchman. They nests fairly early. I've found eggs at the back end o' Febooary. They've got to do summat to proteck theirsels, cos there's no leaves to hide t' nest even now. So they builds the nest like a 'edge'og's skin. The funny thing is that a pair'll build four or five nests sometimes, and only use one on 'em."

In answer to my questioning glance he continued, "I'm not sartain why they mak's such work fer theirsels. P'raps them they don't use is dis'eartners."

"And what in the world are they?" I asked.

"Well," said the old poacher, "if ye climbed up and found two or three big-lookin' nests, and after a deal o' trouble and scratches ye found nowt in 'em, and then ye suddenly saw in another tree a couple more, it ud be nateral fer ye to wonder if it were worth another climb — ye'd be dis'eartened, eh?"

"I should certainly be too disheartened to bother with the second one," I said, feeling the sting of my wounds.

"Well, that's one o' t' reasons why I think them magpies builds so many," said Jerry.

"They are really empty decoys," I said.

"That's 'ow a scholard might describe 'em," said he, with a twinkle in his eyes. "They 'minds me, though, o' them lucky packets we used to buy when we were childer. Owd Martha Bell's mother used to 'ave 'em in t' shop winder, made o' some sort o' soft jujube and dusted wi' white flour or sugar — aboot half t' size o' a small saucer — an' in one on 'em there were said to be a threepenny-bit buried."

"Oh! I remember them — halfpenny each."

Jerry laughed and nodded his head. "Aye, that were t' price, and we used to go in and pick 'em up and when she warn't looking weigh 'em in oor hand to see if we could find t' heaviest. I niver got t' threepenny-bit, and I niver knew nobody as did — them were decoys o' emptiness, I reckon."

"Found any other nests, yet?" I asked as we strode along.

"There's one up t' lane yonder we can look at, It's a thrush's, and t' young uns are a'most ready fer flyin'.'"

From a neighbouring field we heard the bubbling nesting song of a curlew.

"Have you come across her's yet?"

Jerry shook his head. "She won't nest till she's sure t' frost's all over. She's got that bill of 'er's to reckon wi'."

"But so has the thrush," I said, egging him on.

"Aye, but t' thrush 'as a short 'ard beak, an' she can dig a bit wi' it, frost or no frost. But yon curlew's 'as to probe down in t' mud, and if t' ground's 'ard she'll git nowt, I reckon."

We walked on in silence for a few moments. Jerry had given a new turn to my thoughts. I had never thought how the build of a bird affected its early or late nesting habits. I thought of

the early nesters, such as the raven and the wild duck, and mentally was examining their beaks, when I heard Jerry saying, "Here's t' young thrushes."

Raq returned from scouring the bracken to see what we were looking at. The nest lay in the bottom of the hedge and was hardly screened in any way. He put his nose up, but I do not think that they could have given off any scent, for he soon left us and returned to his hunting.

The young birds showed no sign of fear, but lifted their innocent faces with their huge gapes as we put our fingers in. But as soon as the mother bird returned with a worm in her bill, she gave two staccato notes, and the wee mites crouched like clockwork. She had given them a lesson in the art of being afraid. After that, though we snapped our fingers above them, they made no response to our advances.

"I've 'eard 'er mak' t' same noise when a carrion crow 'as bin 'angin' aboot," was the old poacher's comment, "an'," he added, "that's the kind o' trainin' I was telling ye aboot that yon caged bullfinch would miss if 'e were set free."

As we walked up the lane we noticed a robin with its beak full of insects, and it didn't take Jerry very long to find its snug nest tucked away in the bank. There were five young robins in it, and they, too, were almost ready to quit the nest.

"Keep yer eye on 'er and see what she does," said Jerry, taking hold of Raq.

Quite still she stood for a few moments, watching us carefully as we stood some six or seven yards from the nest.

"She's reck'nin' us up," said Jerry; and then gently added, "We're friends, lil' girl, we'll not 'urt yer family."

A moment later she was down discharging her cargo into the hungry throats of her youngsters, returning at once to her former perch to sing a joyous litany.

"She doesn't seem afraid of us," I said; and as though to confirm my words, she flew down to the ground, and with occasional glances at us, searched for more food.

138

"Do you think she was telling the youngsters that there was nothing to fear from the two big giants peering at them?"

"Mebbe," said Jerry. "Ye see, yon robin 'as been man's companion fer centuries, and I reckons if a bird can warn 'er youngsters when to lie low, she ought to be able to tell 'em when there's nowt to fear."

Soon we had left the hedges and the lanes behind, and were crunching our way over the dead brown bracken. Raq was having a great time amongst the young rabbits that were out basking in the sunshine, but as they dashed beneath the undergrowth he could make little headway, and they fooled him easily. I think he must have got hold of one, for I heard a squeal, but I could find no trace of it, so not much damage could have been done.

"Where are you making for, Jerry?" I asked.

For answer he pointed to a big grey rock which was the dividing point of two large ghylls. We clambered up to the top, and shaded from the cold wind, sprawled in the sun's genial warmth.

"This is one o' t' best spots aboot 'ere fer gettin' a bird's-eye-view. Ye can lie doon and watch t' valley, and on both sides ye've got them big dips in t' fells, and there's a'most allus somethin' interestin' goin' on. I was sittin' up 'ere once —"

But Jerry never finished his sentence. I saw him looking intently into the ghyll on our right. He pointed at a big black bird which was flying low over the bracken and heather and whispered, "Raven."

"What is it doing?" I began, but stopped, for Jerry was motioning me to focus my binoculars on it. Every now and then it slackened speed and seemed to be on the point of alighting, but never actually did so.

"It's chasing a rabbit, a youngster," I said, "and the little chap is dashing about trying to take cover under the heather."

"Let's look," said Jerry excitedly, and I passed him the glasses.

"'E's droppin' low an' makin' t' rabbit run. Poor lil' beggar must be far away from 'is burrer. 'E's losin' 'is 'ead wi' fright. 'E's just run under that big black clump."

"The raven is swooping down on his hiding-place just like a hawk does. He's almost swishing the heather with his wings. Look! The rabbit's off again and coming this way, Jerry."

It was a thrilling chase to watch, a mad game of 'hide-and-seek, with a ruthless black devil for the seeker. He gave the rabbit no breathing space. As we watched we soon saw the raven's strategy. He was surely but doggedly "shepherding" his prey towards a large open space where neither bracken nor heather grew, but only the grey rocks peeped through the sparse grass. The rabbit might twist and turn, but the raven gave him no peace until he made him bolt towards that open space.

Now bunny rested a moment in the last patch of cover which fringed the open space. Then the raven swooped once more, and its fierce screech sent bunny speeding out into the open bare ground. For a moment there was a neck-and-neck race. Then the end came swiftly. I could see the cruel black bill give a vicious jab. It struck the rabbit not where I expected, on the head, but on its hind-quarters. Bunny rolled over and over, and another swift jab of the raven's bill put an end to its misery.

"Ham-stringed!" said Jerry.

"What's that?" I asked curtly, for at the moment I was furious with the black murderer, and Jerry did not sound sympathetic.

"Ye saw that jab at t' rabbit's leg. Well, it cut the tendons as neatly as ye could 'ave done it wi' a pair o' scissors. It were a very neat job."

"Clever, perhaps, but cruel," I replied. "Come on, Jerry." I did not relish staying to watch the raven at his feast.

As we walked home a lark overhead was linking together its fairy song chain, and a chaffinch, swaying on a furze bush, poured forth its cheery roundelay.

What heartlessness there seems to be in Nature!

CHAPTER
TWENTY-ONE

Farm Horses

As Raq and I turned towards the open country, in nine out of every ten houses the blinds were still drawn.

"They're all missing the best part of the day, old man, aren't they?" I said to him. For answer he jumped up and touched my fingers with his velvet nose.

The sun was brilliant, and on every field were the long shadows of the trees. How cool their delicate lace-work looked as it fell on the grass! A delicious fragrance arose from a new-mown field as the dew lay on the long swathes. The birds were busy hopping about picking out the insects which swarmed on their stems.

High in the air the swifts wheeled and screamed. I have watched these black-coated migrants for years, but they are still strangers to me. The swallow and the house-martin love to swerve near the haunts of man, and seem ever ready to be friendly with him. Not so the swifts. There is no friendship with them. They live apart, never seeming to sleep, never beholden to any man.

Passing a hole in a tree well known to me, I noticed that a blue-tit had hatched her young family and that the nest was discarded. There had been eleven fluffy mites in it — a sheer case of overcrowding. How they had all managed to breathe is beyond me, for they lay in tiers, and what the bottom row must have endured during the recent hot weather is beyond imagination. What an upheaval took place each time the parent bird returned with food! Those at the bottom forced their way to the top, with open bills. Each return must have caused a miniature earthquake in the nest.

Searching about, I discovered them — little atoms of grey-green, blue and yellow, seated two by two on the

branches of a hawthorn. For a time they snuggled down, finding difficulty in keeping their balance, for their "rudders" were not developed. Then, as they caught sight of the mother-bird returning, there was wild excitement and a fluttering of tiny wings. Each duly received his share of food, though how the

mother managed to carry a bit for each was incredible. And how she remembered who had had their share was likewise a mystery, so like each other were they.

Raq loves the farm, and when I turned up the lane which leads to it, he showed great delight. Joe was in the stable with the lads, who were brushing down the horses before turning them out. It is best done when the horses are dry, to get that lovely sheen which makes them shine like silk.

"How often are they fed?" I asked.

"Three times a day — a bit of hay, some rolled oats, and bran," replied Joe.

Magnificent animals they looked, so suggestive of power. A bull gives me the sense of tremendous strength, but a horse gives me the sense of beauty also — curved strength.

"I do love to see them rolling over on their backs in the field, Joe."

Joe smiled. "Aye, and it's good for 'em an' all. When they've bin workin' an' are turned loose they're ready a'most to begin again if they have a roll. It kind o' relaxes all their muscles and makes 'em fit again."

"Do they lie down when they sleep?"

Joe nodded. "Most on 'em does."

"You find odd uns though, that sleep standing up, don't you, Joe?" said John, who had just come into the stable.

"Do they stand on all fours?" I asked.

They both laughed at this. "Aye, they do," said Joe. "But they tires easily, and their sleep can't do 'em much good. If I bought a horse at a sale, and then found later that 'e went to sleep standin' up, I should return 'im to the feller as sold 'im to me, and he'd have to take him back. We reckons it a fault in a horse, ye see."

"Have you noticed that a horse gets up different from a cow?" John asked.

Glad to show that I knew a little, I said, "Yes, a horse rises by straightening out its fore-legs first, and a cow straightens out its hind legs first."

144

Joe laughed. "There's a good many as couldn't tell ye that, I reckon."

As we left the stable the dogs began to bark, and Sally, Joe's wife, appeared at the back door. It was Ned arriving with the letters, so we all gathered round as he dipped into his bag.

"Not much this mornin'," he said apologetically to Sally.

"Ned," I said, "what's the difference between the way a horse gets up after lying down and the way a cow gets up?"

The old postman chuckled. "Is that a riddle, or do ye really want to know?" he asked. Then, seeing by the smiles that I was having a bit of fun, he said, "Tell me first, 'ow can ye tell 'ow old a 'orse is?"

"By looking at its teeth," I replied promptly.

Joe put his hand on my shoulder and said, "Good fer you. That's reet."

"An' 'ow can ye tell the age of a chicken?" Ned persisted.

"By chewing it," said Joe, much to everyone's amusement.

"By looking at its legs and examining the scales on them," said Sally.

Ned nodded. "An' 'ow can ye tell the age of a tree?"

"By the rings on the cross-section of its trunk," answered John.

Again Ned nodded. "Now I'll ask ye a 'ard one. 'Ow can ye tell the age of a fish?"

Dead silence.

"By its size," I began.

Ned shook his head. "I were sittin' on t' river bank t' other day, an' a chap fishin' were cuttin' oppen a fish 'e'd caught. After we'd chatted a bit aboot state o' t' watter, 'e showed me a small stone. 'Know what it is?' he asked. 'Nay,' says I, 'I don't.' 'It's a otholith,' he said, with the look of satisfaction Ned always showed in using long words. "A otholith," the old postman repeated, and fumbling in his pockets he produced a bit of paper. "I got 'im to write it fer me."

"Well, what is it?" asked Joe.

"It's a stone oot o' the ear of a fish, which wobbles aboot an' tells t' fish whether it is swimmin' right way up or wrong way up — a kind o' balancer, ye see. Well now, accordin' to t' size of t' stone, so ye can tell the age o' t' fish."

"Well, I've learned something this morning," said Sally, with a smile.

"And how do ye tell the age of a woman?" asked Joe, looking slyly at his wife's receding figure.

Ned looked round, then gave one of his driest chuckles. "I reckon there's only one sure way i' these days — 'er birth certificate."

"Just when lamb becomes mutton tak's some decidin'," said Joe, as Ned departed, and we all followed into the kitchen.

★　★　★

"And what's your job to-day, Joe?" I asked. He looked up towards the High Barn, scorched with sunshine.

"Scufflin' turnips."

"You are welcome to it," I said, thinking of the heat, the dry earth, and the unending rows of small plants to be thinned out. "How are they looking?"

"Might be better. T' fly 'as gone wi' some on 'em. Some say the linnets have bothered 'em."

"Linnets?" I exclaimed in amazement. "I've never heard of such a thing."

"Well," said Joe, "they're sayin' roond here that linnets have come doon in flocks and taken away t' seed. If it's true, that's a new enemy we have to watch."

"Have you had to sow some again?"

"Aye, a few, but turnips of a second sowing never do as well as a first."

As I sat in the kitchen and watched Joe and his men get ready for their work and heard their hearty fun and chatter, while Sally filled their bottles with tea for their ten-o'-clocks, and then saw them turn their faces towards High Barn, I could not help feeling that were I given the choice between a City office and going with them up to High Barn, I should choose the latter.

CHAPTER
TWENTY-TWO

The Merlin

"I've got a merlin's nest to show ye," said Jerry. "Ye allus said ye'd like to find one. It's a goodish walk on t' fells — are ye game for a tramp?"

I nodded, though visions of my tiring trudge to the buzzard's ledge rose before me.

"How far is it?" I said.

"Mebbe four miles — more or less," he answered with a grin.

"Mebbe more," I said ruefully, for the day was hot.

"We'll 'ave a bite afore we start," he said, taking it for granted that I should go.

So, giving Raq a bone on the hearth-rug, Jerry made me sit down whilst he fried a most appetizing trout. I watched him dip it in oatmeal, and as it sizzled in the pan, I felt quite hungry.

"How did you catch this, Jerry?" I asked.

"Three guesses," he answered.

"You 'tickled' it?"

He shook his head.

"You snared it, then, with a running noose."

He looked reproachfully at me. "I notice ye didn't ask first if I caught it fair and square wi' rod and line."

148

"Well, then, some angler must have given it to you," I said finally.

"I see you don't think much o' me skill neither. Well, I'll tell ye. I'd bin settin' a few rabbit snares in owd Graham's field doon by t' riverside, fer t' whole place were wick wi' 'em."

"Yes," I said, "I've noticed what a lot there are this year."

Jerry nodded. "Aye, it's bin a grand Spring fer 'em; in fact, it's bin grand weather fer all wild things. I've niver seen more young plovers aboot than this season. Ye see, there's bin no 'eavy rains to droon 'em. Well, as I were sayin', I were tryin' to thin oot owd Graham's rabbits, as they were eatin' 'is young oats summat terrible. Goin' doon to t' field, I noticed an owd yarn (heron) fly up wi' summat in 'er bill. It seemed 'eavy fer 'er to carry far, so she came doon agin in t' field where t' snares was."

"Did she come up from the river?"

"So far as I could see it were from t' river. When I reached t' field I thought t' yarn would git up at once, fer they're awful shy birds, an' their sight is as quick as a 'awk's. But to my surprise I saw 'er try to git up and then fall back to t' ground. She were dancing aboot like a cat on 'ot bricks, and when I got up to 'er I saw she 'ad a trout aside of 'er, but I could 'ardly believe me eyes when I saw that a rabbit were caught in a wire snare, an' t' wire snare were wrapped roon t' yarn's legs so as she couldn't git away."

"What an extraordinary thing!" I exclaimed.

"I reckon t' yarn were flyin' off wi' t' trout when she found it more'n she could manage. So she planed doon, and weren't too pertic'lar where she landed, an' then t' rabbit popped up skeered-like and twined itsel' roond 'er legs afore she knowed what was 'appenin'. So ye see I got a yarn, a trout, and a rabbit in one go. The trout ye're eatin', and t' rabbit went to market wi' t' rest."

"And the yarn?"

"Oh, I let the poor beggar go. I threw me coat ower 'er to get old o' t' trout, fer I didn't want 'er sharp bill in me shins, and she flew away usin' langwidge that nearly cooked t' trout."

Finishing our meal, we walked along the lane which led from Jerry's cottage.

A plover swooped down with noisy wings and an angry shriek at Raq, and to my amazement settled on the road but a few yards ahead of him, with her wings raised as though she were ready to strike at him.

"Call 'im back quick," said Jerry; "she'll 'ave little 'uns near."

So I called and kept him to heel whilst we searched for them. Just where the grass fringed the road we discovered four fluffy little mites cowering under the cover.

"I wonder why she leads them along bare roads where there's so much danger," I said.

"It's 'ard to tell. Mebbe it's 'cos fields is soaked wi' dew first thing i' t' mornin', and t' lane is a nice dry place to walk on. If a young bird gets soaked, then it's easy game fer enemies."

"I should have thought that they were easy game at any time. A young plover can't fly for long. A young sparrow can fly out of harm's way when it's once out of the nest, but a young plover can only run."

"Ye'd change yer tune if ye'd ever tried to chase a young plover. It can run like a 'are, and turn and twist like quicksilver. Then they drops down and 'ides in t' grass, and ye can walk over 'em wi'oot seein' 'em."

We soon left the cultivated fields behind, and were climbing upwards towards the hills, which were covered with long and coarse grass. Here and there a grouse chuckled joyfully, whilst butterflies of varied hues chased each other amongst the tufts of grass.

Going up one small ghyll, Jerry pointed to a lizard about a couple of inches long basking in the sun on the rocks. I crawled carefully to where he dozed, and Raq sidled along as excited as I was. Then I made a grab at him, but when I opened my hand all I had was a part of his tail. Jerry laughed uproariously.

"Ye just missed 'im by an inch. That's a trick of 'is. When 'e feels yer 'and on 'im 'e leaves ye a bit of 'is tail as a consolation prize. Ye'd better stick that bit in yer garden," he added with a grin; "ye might git a whole lizard from that bit of a cuttin'."

"And will he grow another tail?"

Jerry nodded. "Aye, but mebbe not as good a one as 'is first. Still, it'll sarve 'is purpose."

As we climbed higher I told Jerry all about the buzzard's nest which I had visited last week with Joe.

"'Ow many youngsters was there, did ye say?"

"Three."

"Then there's bin no murders committed."

I made no reply, for I knew he would tell me.

"Ye see, when t' buzzard lays 'er first egg, she sits on it straight away — different to a thrush or a finch, as waits till all 'er eggs is laid afore startin' to sit. So ye see t' fust-laid egg 'atches oot afore t'others, an' that day or

WHERE'S EMILY GONE ?

two mak's all t' difference to its size. 'E gets all t' food, and so is as strong as a young bull when 'is brothers and sisters break their shells. Then later, if food is scarce, 'e just turns and mak's a meal o' one o' 'em. So when ye finds only one young 'un in t' nest, t'other two is' — here Jerry pointed to his waistcoat.

"There were several young dead rabbits lying in this buzzard's nest, Jerry."

"There ye are. Plenty o' food means that none of 'em is ever 'ungry enough to turn cannibal."

"It's a cruel business," I said.

"It's Nature's way o' preservin' t' race. There's an instinck i' birds which seems to say, 'If three can't live, then one must — by 'ook or by crook.'"

As we got nearer our destination, Jerry stopped Raq ranging about, and put him on a leash. Then I saw a blue-backed bird shoot up into the air, and on the ground, amongst the heather, we found three fluffy young ones, surrounded by the litter of their meals.

It was the merlin, and from above came her cries of complaint.

"That's where she's different to t' kestrel," said Jerry. "She flies off and leaves t' youngsters to their fate. I reckons if I covers ye up in yon butt, and then walks away, ye may see 'er feed 'em."

So Jerry screened Raq and me in the butt used for grouse-shooting, and then walked off noisily.

"I'll be back in an 'our or so. It would be no use both on us stayin'. She'd know we was there. I reckon ye'll not 'ave long to wait, but it's a pity ye didn't bring yer camera wi' yer."

After nearly an hour of waiting, the falcon appeared, carrying in its mouth a pipit — a small brown bird, rather like a lark. The youngsters rose from the ground to meet her, uttering low cries of expectancy and joy.

She stood on her prey, and pressing her tail against the ground for leverage, drove her bill savagely into the dead bird, and then gave the shreds to her young ones. Then off she went to search for more.

"Did ye see the cock bird an' all?" Jerry asked on his return.

"No, I don't think so. It looked like the same bird every time."

"He's the smaller bird. In all the 'awks ye'll find t' cock is smaller than 'is mate — peregrine or kestrel. P'raps it is that she 'as to do most o' t' work, and so Nature 'as given 'er more wing-power."

"I think I'd rather climb up than down, Jerry," I said, as we started for home.

Jerry laughed. "It does jolt ye up a bit — but a shakin' up o' yer innards is better'n a bottle o' medicine. Come on, Raq! Put yer best leg for'ards, fer, i' my opinion, we're goin' to 'ave a storm. Fells is not t' best place when there's lightnin' aboot."

CHAPTER
TWENTY-THREE

Crusoe and His Man Friday

It was four o'clock in the morning of the merry month of May. The sun was gilding the mill chimneys, and light mist veiled the ugliness of man-made streets. The bonnet of the car was turned towards the North, and at the magic word "Scotland," the motor purred with pleasure towards the open country.

My companion was Rennie, an artist in bird photography. Raq snuggled contentedly amidst a multitudinous assortment of cameras, hiding-tents, plates, billy-cans and sleeping-bags. In our hearts was the song of the open road. In our minds lay a vision of an island promontory, where we knew the sea-birds chanted their raucous melodies, and where invading feet were rare.

We sped through delectable Cumberland, where the curlew greeted us with bubbling song, and the plover side-slipped, pirouetted, and dived like a stunt airman saluting royalty.

Over the bridge that divides England from Scotland we sped, not heeding the lure of the blacksmith's shop, where hasty marriages were made — oft to be repented at leisure.

Then the hills began to rise, Galloway's hills — there are none to compare with them. And though their solitudes beckoned to us, we resisted the temptation, and after seven hours' steady travel, we steamed into a quiet little fishing village where time was not, and where to-morrow was yesterday.

Away in the distance lay the island of our dreams. As soon as we saw it we changed our plans. It had been our intention to stay at the village and to sail across each morning. We held a consultation, and I proposed that we should abandon that idea and set out at once for the island, taking the risk of finding a suitable place to sleep in. Rennie seconded the motion, Raq wagged his stump of a tail, and it was carried *nem. con.*

Going to the village shop we raided it for bread, butter, tea, condensed milk, and a pot of jam, and soon we were in the boat heading for the open sea. Up the silken ribbon of the estuary we floated. Shelducks gazed at us with wary eyes. Dunlin whistled a morning salute. Mallards scolded us for spoiling their sanctuary. Finally, we stepped out

on the rocks that guarded the herring-gulls' secrets — lords of all we surveyed — Crusoe, his man Friday, and Raq.

"And what time will I fetch ye the nicht?" asked the canny boatman.

We told him that we should not need him for nearly a week. He looked at us and repeated his question, thinking that he had misunderstood us. We gave him the same answer.

As he turned the prow of his boat homewards, I caught the sound of a muttered sentence — "A daft pair o' fules!"

We were by this time feeling somewhat tired and empty, but our first duty was to search for a shelter in which to sleep. One side of the island was guarded by cliffs. Their heights sloped downwards towards a beach of shingle. In between lay marsh and lagoon. Here and there were stunted trees. Grey rock peeped out wherever it could.

Fifty yards from the sea, and where the rocks shielded it from sou-west gales, we found a fisherman's hut. It had as much ventilation as protection. It was not exactly clean, but we hailed it with delight, and stuffed its holes with old sacking. Inside, at the far end and raised from the ground, was a plank bed. Rennie and I tossed for this luxury — I lost.

Then, having found our base, we came across some brackish water. Billy-cans were filled, a fire lit, and with our baggage surrounding us we sat down to our first meal.

And what a meal it was — thick hunches of bread and jam, flavoured with the tang of the incoming tide.

As for Rennie, worker in a mill, daily listening to the rattle of four hundred looms, all he could say was, "I wish someone ud gie me a clowt on t' head. Happen I should wakken up."

As for Raq, a thousand new scents were coming to his sensitive nose. Probably he wondered at mortals who could stop to feed whilst such adventures awaited them.

Not far from the hut which we made our headquarters we had noticed an oyster-catcher. On our approach she had slipped over the side of the rocks. Some fifty yards away we saw her mate doing sentry duty.

I had always been keen on photographing this bird, but previously had met with bad luck. Once, after I had found three nests, I had to dismantle two of my hiding-tents, as I feared the birds were so scared that they would desert their eggs. The third bird was bolder, and everything was ready for me to begin operations. Through the night, however, a sheep trailed through the eggs and broke them — and my aspirations.

Raq found the nest lying snugly between two shoulders of rock. Three eggs nestled on the short sea-grass. What a boon to have found it so near to our base!

Without delay we fixed up the "hide." From afar we saw the bird eyeing it and wondering what new growth this was which overlooked her privacy. But the day was hot and she was in no hurry to cover her treasures. We left her to her own devices and began our search for other nests.

★　★　★

Over on the shingle we noticed two birds acting in rather a suspicious manner. Getting under cover and focussing our binoculars on them, we saw that they were ringed plovers. They are only tiny birds, about twice the size of a robin. We knew them by the black crescent which adorned their breasts, and by the plaintive "peep — pe-e-p" which is the distilled essence of silent shores.

As quickly as possible we made our way to the beach, and when we stood still the birds came very near, pretending that they could hardly fly. We knew then that a couple of youngsters, perhaps more, were not very far from us.

The mother bird produced every artifice in her repertoire. Her wings fluttered brokenly by her side. When she found that we were not "taken in" by this trick and that we remained obstinately still, she came within six yards of us, and, turning over on her side, feigned to be dying a lingering death. We shook our heads at her and laughingly said, "No, no; we are too old to be duped like that."

Then we searched in the shingle, picking our steps with great care, for any pebble might turn out to be one of the little fluffy mites for which the mother was willing to risk her life.

We found what we were looking for — a tiny spoonful of grey life squatting on the shingle, still as death and watching our every movement with black shining eyes. There was only one word to describe the downy statue — it was a darling.

But as soon as the eye of the camera was focussed upon it, the mother changed her call, and the inert fluffiness came to life, and we found that with its long legs it could run faster than we could.

Rennie looked after the two youngsters whilst I rushed back for another camera, the first one being unsuitable. He had the time of his life keeping them from separating. He had nothing with which to cover them, and each ran in opposite directions at the same time.

When finally we had exposed a plate or two, the mother called again, and this time we raised no objection to the reuniting of the family party.

So anxious was the mother that, within five yards of us, she received her little ones with open wings. Then, quite contentedly, she cuddled them under her downy breast, and with a defiant look in her beautiful eyes, she dared us to do our worst. Oh! the marvel of motherhood!

By this time the light was failing, and so we could do no more. Finding a few sacks in the hut, we stuffed them with dry sea-wrack — anything soft which the sea had cast up on the beach. This made our bed. Inside the hut a candle stuck in a bottle did duty for a chandelier. For supper, instead of bread and jam, we had jam and bread. It was Rennie's turn to have the knife. In the corner we found an old stove which would have made a priceless smoke-screen for the Navy. We also unearthed two plates.

Outside the sea was murmuring its quiet undertone of restless joy. Overhead the Great Bear twinkled in an indigo sky. One by one the chuckles of the black-backed gulls sank to silence, as they watched the wavelets rimmed with phosphorescent flame trip up the beach.

Then Rennie turned in on to his bunk. I slept underneath him, with Raq forming a hot-water bottle for my feet. He blinked at me, tired out with chasing rabbits, and every contented blink said, "This is life."

Next morning Rennie said he felt sore from the effects of his hard bed. Several times during the night I had prodded him vigorously with a tent-peg when he produced more melody than I cared for.

Next day the wind was so boisterous that though the oyster-catcher had returned to her nest, photography was out of the question. The gale rocked the tent from side to side, but the bird faced the fearsome flapping terror valiantly.

Away upon the cliff top I caught sight of a white spot. I watched it through my glasses. The white spot sometimes disappeared, and then returned to the same place.

In great heat Rennie and I climbed up, and to our delight found the nest of the common gull with three eggs in it. Then we walked about a mile for our paraphernalia, set up our hiding-tent, and had the satisfaction of seeing the bird return easily to the nest.

This bird with an unpromising name only nests in about three places in Great Britain. What luck to have come across her in this remote sanctuary!

I risked entering the tent at once. Rennie took up a position a mile from me, where he watched proceedings through his binoculars. Without showing much fear the bird took up her duties about a quarter of an hour after I had entered the tent. She was a bold mother.

Never shall I forget the heat of that cramped shelter. My knees propped up my chin. Down them little cascades of perspiration trickled from my brow. I was a six-foot man squeezed into a two foot six square tent, with cameras and plates besides.

Very cautiously I took off my shirt. Then I wriggled out of my knee-breeches, arms and legs having to work in reverse gear. I was still so hot that I threw off the last vestiges of civilization, and like the prodigal, "came to myself."

The cock bird sat immobile on a rock some twenty yards from the nest. From it he could survey the whole sweep of the island. Suddenly he gave a squawk and both birds launched themselves into the air. Looking through my spy-hole I saw them following something that sped through the long grass. They dived at it, swore at it and side-tracked it from the direct line of the nest. It was a stoat, and even he dare not face those enraged gulls.

Soon after they were once more up in the air to face another foe, and we witnessed a battle-royal between them and invading carrion crows. The latter were glad to beat a hasty retreat. A sitting-bird's life is by no means a life of indolence.

The days were passing crowded with glorious free life. We were getting rather tired of jam and bread, and had not much left even of this. In the hut I found a bit of brass wire, and, very loth to do it, I left it set in a rabbit's track — even as I had seen Jerry do. Next morning I found, with a certain amount of regret, that a busy-body bunny had twisted himself up in it. At the sight of a new dish for dinner, Rennie's eyes stood out like organ-stops. I had to clean the beast, and I have never known a rabbit so loth to part with his skin. He was an old buck, and I should think had been a pet of the Romans.

After stewing him in our billy-can for two hours he still would not allow a knife to penetrate any portion of his body. We left him still stewing, and went away to photograph more birds.

Rennie covered me up in a hiding-tent close to where a snipe had her nest. I waited for four hours for the bird to return. It was marshy ground and the water kept oozing into my remoter parts, whilst the stench of the mud at times turned me dizzy.

The bird never appeared, but buoyed up by the

163

knowledge that we were to have rabbit for supper, we tramped joyfully towards the hut.

The billy-can still simmered on the stove, but the rabbit had disappeared, leaving but his taste behind in the water. Six hours' steady boiling had been too much for him! We searched diligently for his flesh, but found only framework. Yet that soup was the sweetest dish that we have ever tasted, and Raq voted that the bones had a relish all their own.

Next day we had better luck, for I left a line and a hook in the sea, and a fish took a fancy to the hook, and we took a fancy to the fish. The next day we faced bread-and-jam, and jam-and-bread — which was by this time showing signs of wear and tear.

And so the hours passed in joyous work, but let no one think that bird photography is an easy pastime. There are hours of tramping and climbing with heavy impedimenta, and inside the tent, keenness alone will bring prized negatives.

But what a joy to wake up with no letters to answer and with no paper to tell of the doings of a hectic world! Sometimes one wished that one could know how things were going on at home. Sometimes a passing boat would see two solitary figures standing on a rock and would wave a cheery salute.

Once, on returning from our usual occupation, we found on the rocks near the hut a parcel. We opened it and found bread, butter and — oh joy — a rasher or two of bacon and some eggs. Like the Israelites we murmured, "It is manna." Some kind soul in the fishing village had thought of us, and the fisherman had left it where he was sure we should find it.

And now Rennie is back at his loom, and I am back in the city. A few weeks ago he came over to see me. When eventide came on we drew up by my study fire and pipes began to glow. Raq snuggled in between us.

Over my mantelpiece hang four pictures. Rennie enlarged them for me. A gull as trim as a white yacht is looking over a valley from the high point on which her eggs lie warm in the sun. The oyster-catcher with her beautiful pied plumage, walks with parsonic gravity towards her home.

For a while we are back at the hut again. Once again we hear the slumbrous moan of mighty waters, see the flash of white wings as we invade the sanctuary of the birds.

So we live over again some of our adventures, the half of which will never be told. And as we talk of that free life Rennie clasps my hand and says, "We mun have another turn next year." And Raq, putting up his paw on my knee, looks gravely at us both, and his tail wags, "Carried unanimously."

Golden Sheaves, Black Horses

Fred Archer

A wonderful memoir of times long past from the celebrated chronicler of life in rural England

"A delight. For ripe rustic nostalgia Fred Archer leaves the field standing." **The Sunday Telegraph**

"I have enjoyed them all but this is probably his best." **The Sunday Times**

A wonderful memoir of times long past from the celebrated chronicler of life in rural England.

In *Golden Sheaves, Black Horses*, Archer has recorded the beauty of the West of England and the life of the villagers living in the area during the last decades of the 19th century.

Archer explained his decision to write about these stubborn and strong characters by saying: "I felt it would be such a pity if, when these characters died, their sayings, customs, ways of life, how they dressed, should vanish with them." Thanks to his powers of observation, memory and, above all, his truthful turn of phrase, they never will.

ISBN 0-7531-9960-2 (hb)
ISBN 0-7531-9961-0 (pb)

A Romany in the Country

G. Bramwell Evens

From 1932 to his death in 1943, George Bramwell Evens captivated audiences up to 13 million with his BBC Children's Hour programme, "Out with Romany". His deep, soothing voice transported listeners everywhere on countryside walks, observing animals and plants alike. Not only a radio voice, he also wrote weekly articles for several papers, for 23 years in some cases.

In *A Romany in the Country*, he shares his knowledge of nature lore — how animals communicate, the lengths to which birds go to build their nests and the marvels of ears — as well as the friends he meets in the lanes and fields. There is Ned, the old postman, a philosopher and poet; Alan and Joe, large-hearted, generous farmers; and Jerry and John, the poacher and the gamekeeper who hold each other in mutual respect.

This is an enlightening read from the nation's first Natural History broadcaster.

ISBN 0-7531-9742-1 (hb)
ISBN 0-7531-9743-X (pb)